THE
Soup Bible

Publications International, Ltd.

TABLE OF CONTENTS

BEEF & PORK

Sausage and Lentil Soup

8 ounces spicy Italian sausage

1 onion, chopped

2 cloves garlic, minced

1 stalk celery, chopped

1 carrot, chopped

1 small zucchini, chopped

3 to 3½ cups chicken broth, divided

1 can (about 14 ounces) diced tomatoes

1 cup dried lentils, rinsed and sorted

½ teaspoon salt

½ teaspoon dried oregano

½ teaspoon dried basil

¼ teaspoon dried thyme

¼ teaspoon black pepper

Chopped fresh basil and grated Parmesan cheese (optional)

1. Brown sausage in large saucepan or Dutch oven over medium-high heat, stirring to break up meat. Add onion; cook and stir 3 minutes or until onion begins to soften. Add garlic; cook and stir 1 minute. Add celery, carrot and zucchini; cook 3 minutes, stirring occasionally.

2. Stir in 3 cups broth, tomatoes, lentils, salt, oregano, dried basil, thyme and pepper; bring to a boil. Reduce heat to low; cover and simmer about 1 hour or until lentils are tender. Add additional broth if needed to thin soup. Garnish with fresh basil and cheese.

Makes 4 to 6 servings

Italian-Style Meatball Soup

½ pound ground beef

¼ pound bulk Italian sausage

1 onion, finely chopped, divided

⅓ cup plain dry bread crumbs

1 egg

½ teaspoon salt

4 cups canned beef broth

2 cups water

1 can (about 8 ounces) stewed tomatoes

1 can (8 ounces) pizza sauce

2 cups sliced cabbage

1 can (about 15 ounces) kidney beans, rinsed and drained

2 carrots, sliced

½ cup frozen Italian green beans

1. Combine beef, sausage, 2 tablespoons onion, bread crumbs, egg and salt in large bowl; mix until well blended. Shape into 32 (1-inch) meatballs.

2. Brown half of meatballs in large skillet over medium heat, turning frequently. Remove from skillet; drain on paper towels. Repeat with remaining meatballs.

3. Bring broth, water, tomatoes and pizza sauce to a boil in Dutch oven over medium-high heat. Add meatballs, remaining onion, cabbage, beans and carrots; bring to a boil. Reduce heat to medium-low; simmer 20 minutes. Add green beans; simmer 10 minutes.

Makes 8 servings

Split Pea Soup

1 package (16 ounces) dried green or yellow split peas

7 cups water

1 pound smoked ham hocks *or* 4 ounces smoked sausage links, sliced and quartered

2 carrots, chopped

1 onion, chopped

¾ teaspoon salt

½ teaspoon dried basil

¼ teaspoon dried oregano

¼ teaspoon black pepper

1. Rinse split peas thoroughly in colander under cold running water; discard any debris or blemished peas.

2. Combine peas, water, ham hocks, carrots, onion, salt, basil, oregano and pepper in large saucepan or Dutch oven; bring to a boil over high heat. Reduce heat to medium-low; simmer 1 hour 15 minutes or until peas are tender, stirring occasionally. Stir frequently near end of cooking to keep soup from scorching.

3. Remove ham hocks; let stand until cool enough to handle. Remove ham from hocks; chop meat and discard bones.

4. Place 3 cups soup in blender or food processor; blend until smooth. Return to saucepan; stir in ham. If soup is too thick, add water until desired consistency is reached. Cook just until heated through.

Makes 6 servings

TIP: To purée soup, carefully pour the hot mixture into the blender. Cover with the lid, removing the center cap, then cover the hole with a towel. Start blending at low speed and gradually increase to high speed, blending to desired consistency.

Classic Meatball Soup

2 pounds beef bones

3 stalks celery

2 carrots

1 medium onion, cut in half

1 bay leaf

6 cups cold water

1 egg

4 tablespoons chopped fresh parsley, divided

1 teaspoon salt, divided

½ teaspoon dried marjoram leaves, crushed

¼ teaspoon black pepper, divided

½ cup soft fresh bread crumbs

¼ cup grated Parmesan cheese

1 pound ground beef

1 can (about 14 ounces) diced tomatoes

½ cup uncooked rotini or small elbow macaroni

1. To make stock, rinse bones and combine with celery, carrots, onion and bay leaf in 6-quart stockpot. Add water. Bring to a boil; reduce heat to low. Cover partially and simmer 1 hour, skimming foam occasionally.

2. Preheat oven to 400°F. Spray 13×9-inch baking pan with nonstick cooking spray. Combine egg, 3 tablespoons parsley, ½ teaspoon salt, marjoram and ⅛ teaspoon pepper in medium bowl; whisk lightly. Stir in bread crumbs and cheese. Add beef; mix well. Place meat mixture on cutting board; pat evenly into 1-inch-thick square. With sharp knife, cut meat into 1-inch squares; shape each square into a ball. Place meatballs in prepared pan; bake 20 to 25 minutes until brown on all sides and cooked through, turning occasionally. Drain on paper towels.

3. Strain stock through sieve into medium bowl. Slice celery and carrots; reserve. Remove and discard bones, onion and bay leaf. To degrease stock, let stand 5 minutes to allow fat to rise. Holding paper towel, quickly pull across surface only, allowing towel to absorb fat. Discard. Repeat with clean paper towels as many times as needed to remove all fat.

4. Return stock to stockpot. Drain tomatoes, reserving juice. Chop tomatoes; add to stock with juice. Bring to a boil; boil 5 minutes. Stir in rotini, remaining ½ teaspoon salt and ⅛ teaspoon pepper. Cook 6 minutes, stirring occasionally. Add reserved vegetables and meatballs. Reduce heat to medium; cook 10 minutes or until pasta is done. Stir in remaining 1 tablespoon parsley. Season to taste.

Makes 4 to 6 servings

Italian Wedding Soup

1 tablespoon olive oil

1 pound bulk Italian sausage*

½ cup chopped onion

½ cup chopped carrots

1 teaspoon Italian seasoning

7½ cups reduced-sodium chicken broth

3 cups packed coarsely chopped kale

1 cup uncooked ditalini or other small shaped pasta

Grated Parmesan cheese (optional)

If bulk sausage is not available, use sausage links and remove the casings.

1. Heat oil in Dutch oven or large saucepan over medium-high heat. Add sausage, onion, carrots and Italian seasoning; cook and stir about 4 minutes or until sausage is cooked through. Drain fat.

2. Stir in broth and kale; bring to a boil over high heat. Stir in pasta. Reduce heat to medium-low; simmer, partially covered, about 9 minutes or until pasta is tender. Sprinkle with Parmesan.

Makes 6 servings

Beef Goulash Soup with Caraway

1 teaspoon canola oil

1¼ pounds boneless beef sirloin tri-tip roast,* cut into 1-inch pieces

1 cup chopped onion

3 cans (about 14 ounces each) reduced-sodium beef broth

2 cans (about 14 ounces each) diced tomatoes

1½ cups sliced carrots

2 tablespoons sugar

1 tablespoon paprika

1 tablespoon caraway seeds, slightly crushed

2 cloves garlic, minced

4 ounces (about 2 cups) uncooked whole wheat noodles

2 cups thinly sliced cabbage or coleslaw mix

Substitute chuck roast or beef round steak, if desired.

1. Heat oil in nonstick Dutch oven over medium heat. Brown beef in 2 batches; transfer to paper towel-lined plate. Drain fat. Add onion; cook 3 minutes or until onion is tender, stirring occasionally.

2. Return beef to Dutch oven. Add broth, tomatoes, carrots, sugar, paprika, caraway seeds and garlic; bring to a boil. Reduce heat to medium-low. Cover; simmer 45 minutes or until beef is tender.

3. Stir in noodles; bring to a boil. Reduce heat to medium-low; simmer, uncovered, 10 minutes or until noodles are tender. Stir in cabbage; cook 2 minutes or until heated through.

Makes 8 to 9 servings

Sweet Potato and Ham Soup

1 tablespoon butter

1 leek, sliced

1 clove garlic, minced

4 cups reduced-sodium chicken broth

2 sweet potatoes, peeled and cut into ¾-inch cubes

½ pound ham, cut into ½-inch cubes

½ teaspoon dried thyme

2 ounces stemmed spinach, coarsely chopped

1. Melt butter in large saucepan over medium heat. Add leek and garlic; cook and stir until tender.

2. Add broth, sweet potatoes, ham and thyme; bring to a boil over high heat. Reduce heat to low; simmer 10 minutes or until sweet potatoes are tender.

3. Stir spinach into soup; cook 2 minutes or until wilted. Serve immediately.

Makes 6 servings

New Orleans Pork Gumbo

1 pound pork tenderloin

1 tablespoon butter

2 tablespoons all-purpose flour

1 cup water

1 can (16 ounces) stewed
  tomatoes, undrained

1 package (10 ounces) frozen cut
  okra

1 package (10 ounces) frozen
  succotash

1 cube beef bouillon

1 teaspoon black pepper

1 teaspoon hot pepper sauce

1 bay leaf

1. Cut pork into ½-inch cubes. Spray large Dutch oven with nonstick cooking spray. Heat over medium heat until hot. Add pork; cook and stir 4 minutes or until pork is browned. Remove pork from Dutch oven.

2. Melt butter in same Dutch oven. Stir in flour. Cook and stir until mixture is dark brown but not burned. Gradually whisk in water until smooth. Add pork and remaining ingredients. Bring to a boil. Reduce heat to low; simmer 15 minutes. Remove and discard bay leaf.

Makes 4 servings

Oxtail Soup with Beer

2½ pounds oxtails (beef or veal)

1 large onion, sliced

4 carrots, cut into 1-inch pieces, divided

3 stalks celery, cut into 1-inch pieces, divided

2 sprigs fresh parsley

5 whole black peppercorns

1 bay leaf

4 cups beef broth

1 cup dark beer

2 cups diced baking potatoes

1 teaspoon salt

2 tablespoons chopped fresh parsley (optional)

1. Combine oxtails, onion, half of carrots, one third of celery, parsley sprigs, peppercorns and bay leaf in large saucepan. Add broth and beer; bring to a boil over high heat. Reduce heat to low; cover and simmer 3 hours or until meat is falling off bones.

2. Remove oxtails to plate; set aside. Strain broth and return to saucepan; skim fat. Add remaining carrots, celery and potatoes; bring to a simmer. Cook 10 to 15 minutes or until vegetables are tender.

3. Remove meat from oxtails; discard bones. Stir meat and salt into soup; cook until heated through. Remove and discard bay leaf. Sprinkle with chopped parsley, if desired.

Makes 4 servings

Vegetable Beef Noodle Soup

8 ounces beef for stew, cut into ½-inch pieces

¾ cup unpeeled cubed potato (1 medium)

½ cup sliced carrot

1 tablespoon balsamic vinegar

¾ teaspoon dried thyme

¼ teaspoon black pepper

2½ cups fat-free reduced-sodium beef broth

1 cup water

¼ cup chili sauce or ketchup

2 ounces uncooked thin egg noodles

¾ cup jarred or canned pearl onions, rinsed and drained

¼ cup frozen peas

1. Spray large saucepan with nonstick cooking spray; heat over medium-high heat. Add beef; cook 3 minutes or until browned on all sides, stirring occasionally. Remove to plate.

2. Add potato, carrot, vinegar, thyme and pepper to saucepan; cook and stir over medium heat 3 minutes. Add broth, water and chili sauce. Bring to a boil over medium-high heat; add beef. Reduce heat to medium-low; cover and simmer 30 minutes or until meat is almost fork-tender.

3. Bring beef mixture to a boil over medium-high heat. Add noodles; cover and cook 7 to 10 minutes or until noodles are tender, stirring occasionally. Add onions and peas; cook 1 minute or until heated through. Serve immediately.

Makes 6 servings

Tortellini Soup

½ pound mild or hot Italian sausage links, in casings

½ cup water

1 tablespoon olive oil

1 medium onion, chopped

2 cloves garlic, minced

4 cups reduced-sodium beef broth

1 can (about 14 ounces) whole tomatoes, drained, chopped

1 carrot, sliced

1 teaspoon dried oregano leaves, crushed

1 teaspoon dried basil

½ teaspoon salt

¼ teaspoon black pepper

1 small zucchini, halved, sliced

1 package (9 ounces) refrigerated, cheese-filled tortellini*

Grated Parmesan cheese

Do not use frozen tortellini.

1. Cook sausage in medium skillet over medium heat 7 minutes or until evenly browned, turning occasionally. Add water. Reduce heat to low; cover and simmer 20 minutes. Drain; allow sausage to stand at room temperature until cool enough to handle.

2. Heat oil in 5-quart Dutch oven over medium heat. Cook and stir onion and garlic in oil 4 minutes or until onion is soft.

3. Stir in broth, tomatoes, carrot, oregano, basil, salt and pepper. Bring to a boil over high heat. Reduce heat to medium-low; simmer, uncovered, 30 minutes, stirring occasionally.

4. Cut sausage into thin slices; add to Dutch oven. Simmer 10 minutes. Bring soup to a boil over high heat. Add zucchini and tortellini; cook over medium-high heat 7 minutes or until pasta is just tender. Ladle into bowls. Sprinkle each serving with cheese; serve immediately.

Makes 6 servings

NOTE: Tortellini continues to absorb liquid while standing. It may be necessary to add additional broth when reheating soup.

Beefy Broccoli & Cheese Soup

¼ pound ground beef

2 cups beef broth

1 bag (10 ounces) frozen chopped broccoli, thawed

¼ cup chopped onion

1 cup milk

2 tablespoons all-purpose flour

1 cup (4 ounces) shredded sharp Cheddar cheese

1½ teaspoons chopped fresh oregano *or* ½ teaspoon dried oregano

Salt and black pepper

Hot pepper sauce

1. Brown beef in large skillet over medium-high heat 6 to 8 minutes, stirring to break up meat. Drain fat.

2. Pour broth into medium saucepan; bring to a boil over medium-high heat. Add broccoli and onion; cook 5 minutes or until broccoli is tender. Stir milk into flour in small bowl until smooth. Stir milk mixture and ground beef into saucepan; cook and stir until mixture is thickened and heated through.

3. Add cheese and oregano; stir until cheese is melted. Season with salt, black pepper and hot pepper sauce.

Makes 4 servings

Beef Soup with Noodles

2 tablespoons soy sauce

1 teaspoon minced fresh ginger

¼ teaspoon red pepper flakes

1 boneless beef top sirloin steak (about ¾ pound)

1 tablespoon peanut or vegetable oil

2 cups sliced mushrooms

2 cans (about 14 ounces each) beef broth

1 cup (3 ounces) fresh snow peas, cut diagonally into 1-inch pieces

1½ cups hot cooked egg noodles (2 ounces uncooked)

1 green onion, cut diagonally into thin slices

1 teaspoon dark sesame oil (optional)

Red bell pepper strips (optional)

1. Combine soy sauce, ginger and red pepper flakes in small bowl. Pour mixture evenly over both sides of steak. Marinate 15 minutes.

2. Heat peanut oil in deep skillet over medium-high heat. Drain steak; reserve marinade (there will only be a small amount of marinade). Add steak to skillet; cook 5 minutes per side or until desired doneness. Remove to large cutting board; let stand 10 minutes to cool slightly.

3. Meanwhile, add mushrooms to skillet; stir-fry 2 minutes. Add broth, snow peas and reserved marinade; bring to a boil, scraping up any browned bits from bottom of skillet. Reduce heat to medium-low. Stir in noodles.

4. Cut steak lengthwise in half, then crosswise into thin slices. Stir into soup; heat through. Stir in green onion and sesame oil, if desired. Ladle soup into bowls; garnish with bell pepper strips, if desired.

Makes 4 servings

Stir-Fry Beef & Vegetable Soup

1 boneless beef top sirloin or top round steak (about 1 pound)

2 teaspoons dark sesame oil, divided

3 cans (about 14 ounces each) reduced-sodium beef broth

1 package (16 ounces) frozen stir-fry vegetables

3 green onions, thinly sliced

¼ cup stir-fry sauce

1. Slice beef lengthwise in half, then crosswise into ⅛-inch-thick strips.

2. Heat 1 teaspoon sesame oil in large saucepan or Dutch oven over medium-high heat; tilt pan to coat bottom. Add half of beef in single layer. Cook 1 minute, without stirring, until lightly browned on bottom. Turn and cook other side about 1 minute. Remove beef from pan. Repeat with remaining 1 teaspoon sesame oil and beef; set aside.

3. Add broth to saucepan. Cover; bring to a boil over high heat. Add vegetables. Reduce heat; simmer 3 to 5 minutes or until vegetables are heated through. Add beef, green onions and stir-fry sauce; simmer 1 minute.

Makes 6 servings

SERVING SUGGESTION: Make a quick sesame bread to serve with this soup. Brush refrigerated dinner roll dough with water, then dip in sesame seeds before baking.

Sausage Vegetable Rotini Soup

1 tablespoon olive oil

6 ounces bulk pork sausage

1 cup chopped onion

1 cup chopped green bell pepper

3 cups water

1 can (about 14 ounces) diced
  tomatoes

¼ cup ketchup

2 teaspoons beef bouillon granules

2 teaspoons chili powder

4 ounces uncooked tri-colored
  rotini pasta

1 cup frozen corn, thawed and
  drained

1. Heat oil in large saucepan over medium-high heat. Add sausage; cook 3 minutes or until no longer pink, stirring to break up sausage. Drain fat. Add onion and bell pepper; cook and stir 3 to 4 minutes or until onion is translucent.

2. Add water, tomatoes, ketchup, beef bouillon and chili powder; bring to a boil over high heat. Stir in pasta; return to a boil. Reduce heat to medium-low; simmer, uncovered, 12 minutes. Stir in corn; cook 2 minutes or until pasta is tender and corn is heated through.

Makes 4 servings

Chunky Ancho Chili with Beans

5 dried ancho chiles

2 cups water

2 tablespoons lard or vegetable oil

1 onion, chopped

2 cloves garlic, minced

1 pound boneless beef top sirloin steak, cut into 1-inch cubes

1 pound boneless pork, cut into 1-inch cubes

1 to 2 fresh or canned jalapeño peppers,* stemmed, seeded and minced

1 teaspoon salt

1 teaspoon dried oregano

1 teaspoon ground cumin

½ cup dry red wine

3 cups cooked pinto beans *or* 2 cans (about 15 ounces each) pinto or kidney beans, rinsed and drained

Jalapeño peppers can sting and irritate the skin, so wear rubber gloves when handling peppers and do not touch your eyes.

1. Rinse ancho chiles; remove stems, seeds and veins. Place in medium saucepan with water. Bring to a boil; turn off heat and let stand, covered, 30 minutes or until chiles are soft. Pour chiles with liquid into blender or food processor; process until smooth.

2. Melt lard in 5-quart Dutch oven over medium heat. Add onion and garlic; cook until onion is tender. Add beef and pork; cook, stirring frequently, until meat is lightly browned. Add jalapeño peppers, salt, oregano, cumin, wine and ancho chile purée. Bring to a boil. Cover; reduce heat and simmer 1½ to 2 hours or until meat is very tender. Stir in beans. Simmer, uncovered, 30 minutes or until chili has thickened slightly.

Makes 8 servings

VARIATION: To make chili with chili powder, use ⅓ cup chili powder and 1½ cups water in place of ancho chile purée. Reduce salt and cumin to ½ teaspoon each.

Picante Black Bean Soup

4 slices bacon

1 large onion, chopped

1 clove garlic, minced

2 cans (about 15 ounces each) black beans, undrained

1 can (about 14 ounces) beef broth

1¼ cups water

¾ cup picante sauce

½ teaspoon salt

½ teaspoon dried oregano

Sour cream

Crackers and additional picante sauce for serving

1. Using scissors, cut through several slices of bacon at once, cutting into ½×½-inch pieces.

2. Cook and stir bacon in large saucepan over medium-high heat until crisp. Remove with slotted spoon; drain on paper towels. Set bacon aside.

3. Add onion and garlic to drippings in saucepan; cook and stir 3 minutes.

4. Add beans with liquid, broth, water, ¾ cup picante sauce, salt and oregano. Reduce heat to low. Simmer, covered, 20 minutes.

5. Ladle into soup bowls; dollop with sour cream. Sprinkle with bacon. Serve with crackers and additional picante sauce.

Makes 6 to 8 servings

Pasta and Bean Soup

1¼ cups dried navy beans

6 cups cold water

3 slices bacon, finely chopped

1 onion, chopped

1 stalk celery, chopped

¾ pound smoked pork rib or neck bones

2 cloves garlic, minced

½ teaspoon dried thyme

½ teaspoon dried marjoram

¼ teaspoon black pepper

¾ cup uncooked small pasta shells

2 tablespoons chopped fresh parsley

Salt

1 cup beef broth (optional)

Grated Parmesan cheese

1. Rinse beans well in colander under cold running water, picking out any debris or blemished beans. Combine beans and water in large saucepan. To quick soak beans, bring to a boil over high heat; boil 2 minutes. Remove from heat; cover and let stand 1 hour. **Do not drain**.

2. Cook bacon in medium skillet over medium-high heat 2 minutes. Add onion and celery; cook and stir 6 minutes or until golden brown. Remove bacon, onion and celery to plate; drain off drippings.

3. Rinse pork bones; add to saucepan with beans and soaking water. Stir in bacon mixture, garlic, thyme, marjoram and pepper; bring to a boil over high heat. Reduce heat to medium-low; cook 1 hour or until beans are tender, stirring occasionally. Remove from heat.

4. Remove pork bones to plate; set aside to cool. Transfer half of bean mixture to food processor or blender with slotted spoon. Add 2 tablespoons liquid from soup; process until smooth.

5. Stir puréed bean mixture back into soup; bring to a boil over high heat. Stir in pasta. Reduce heat to medium-low; cook 10 minutes or until pasta is tender, stirring occasionally.

6. Meanwhile, remove meat from bones; discard bones. Chop pork into bite-size pieces. Stir pork and parsley into soup; season with salt. If soup is too thick, add broth until desired consistency is reached. Sprinkle with cheese.

Makes 6 servings

Beef and Vegetable Barley Soup

1 tablespoon vegetable oil

1 to 1½ pounds beef shank cross-cuts

2 medium onions, divided

6 cups water

2 parsnips, peeled and chopped

4 stalks celery, chopped and divided

6 sprigs fresh parsley

6 black peppercorns

2 teaspoons salt

½ pound fresh green beans, cut into 1-inch pieces

4 medium carrots, cut diagonally into ¼-inch-thick slices

½ cup uncooked quick-cooking barley

¼ teaspoon dried tarragon

¼ teaspoon black pepper

1 bay leaf

½ cup frozen corn

½ cup frozen peas

½ cup chopped fresh parsley

1. Heat oil in Dutch oven over medium-high heat. Add beef; cook and stir until browned. Remove from heat.

2. Trim top and root from 1 onion, leaving most of the dried outer skin intact; cut into wedges.

3. Add water, onion wedges, parsnips, half of celery, parsley sprigs, peppercorns and salt to Dutch oven. Bring to a boil over high heat. Reduce heat to medium-low; simmer, uncovered, 1½ hours or until meat is tender, skimming foam that rises to the surface.

4. Remove beef from stock and let cool slightly. Strain stock through large sieve or colander set over large saucepan. Press vegetables lightly with slotted spoon to remove extra liquid; discard vegetables. Let stand 5 minutes to allow fat to rise. Skim off fat and discard.

5. Chop remaining onion. Add chopped onion and remaining celery, green beans, carrots, barley, tarragon, pepper and bay leaf to stock. Bring to a boil over high heat. Reduce heat to medium-low; simmer, uncovered, 15 minutes or until vegetables and barley are tender.

6. Meanwhile, cut meat from bones; discard bones and gristle. Cut meat into bite-size pieces. Stir meat, corn and peas into soup; bring mixture to a boil. Remove and discard bay leaf. Stir in chopped parsley.

Makes 6 servings

Hearty Beefy Beer Soup

1 tablespoon vegetable oil

¾ pound boneless beef round steak, cut into ½-inch pieces

1 large onion, chopped

2 medium carrots, sliced

2 stalks celery, diced

5 cups canned beef broth

1 bottle (12 ounces) stout or dark ale

¾ teaspoon dried oregano

¼ teaspoon salt

⅛ teaspoon black pepper

1 can (about 15 ounces) kidney beans, rinsed and drained

1 small zucchini, cut into ½-inch cubes

4 ounces mushrooms, sliced

1. Heat oil in 5-quart Dutch oven over medium heat. Add beef, onion, carrots and celery. Cook and stir until beef is no longer pink and carrots and celery are crisp-tender.

2. Stir in broth, stout, oregano, salt and pepper. Bring to a boil over high heat. Reduce heat to medium-low; simmer, uncovered, 45 minutes or until beef is fork-tender.

3. Stir beans, zucchini and mushrooms into soup. Bring to a boil over high heat. Reduce heat to medium-low; simmer, uncovered, 5 minutes or until zucchini is tender. Ladle into bowls.

Makes 6 servings

Ground Beef, Spinach and Barley Soup

12 ounces 95% lean ground beef

4 cups water

1 can (about 14 ounces) stewed tomatoes

1½ cups thinly sliced carrots

1 cup chopped onion

½ cup uncooked quick-cooking barley

1½ teaspoons beef bouillon granules

1½ teaspoons dried thyme

1 teaspoon dried oregano

½ teaspoon garlic powder

¼ teaspoon black pepper

⅛ teaspoon salt

3 cups fresh spinach leaves

1. Brown beef in large saucepan over medium-high heat 6 to 8 minutes, stirring to break up meat. Rinse beef under warm water; drain.

2. Return beef to saucepan; stir in 4 cups water, tomatoes, carrots, onion, barley, bouillon, thyme, oregano, garlic powder, pepper and salt; bring to a boil over high heat.

3. Reduce heat to medium-low. Cover; simmer 12 to 15 minutes or until barley and vegetables are tender, stirring occasionally. Stir in spinach; cook until spinach starts to wilt.

Makes 4 servings

Hearty Tuscan Soup

1 teaspoon olive oil

1 pound bulk mild or hot Italian sausage*

1 medium onion, chopped

3 cloves garlic, minced

¼ cup all-purpose flour

5 cups chicken broth

1 teaspoon salt

½ teaspoon Italian seasoning

3 medium unpeeled russet potatoes (about 1 pound), halved lengthwise and thinly sliced

2 cups packed torn stemmed kale leaves

1 cup half-and-half or heavy cream

Or use sausage links and remove from casings.

1. Heat oil in large saucepan or Dutch oven over medium-high heat. Add sausage; cook until sausage begins to brown, stirring to break up meat. Add onion and garlic; cook about 5 minutes or until onion is softened and sausage is browned, stirring occasionally.

2. Stir in flour until blended. Add broth, salt and Italian seasoning; bring to a boil. Stir in potatoes and kale. Reduce heat to medium-low; cook 15 to 20 minutes or until potatoes are fork-tender. Reduce heat to low; stir in cream. Cook about 5 minutes or until heated through.

Makes 6 to 8 servings

Beef Barley Soup

¾ pound boneless beef top round steak, trimmed and cut into ½-inch pieces

3 cans (about 14 ounces each) fat-free reduced-sodium beef broth*

2 cups unpeeled cubed potatoes

1 can (about 14 ounces) no-salt-added diced tomatoes

1 cup chopped onion

1 cup sliced carrots

½ cup uncooked pearl barley

1 tablespoon cider vinegar

2 teaspoons caraway seeds

2 teaspoons dried marjoram

2 teaspoons dried thyme

½ teaspoon salt

½ teaspoon black pepper

1½ cups sliced green beans (½-inch slices)

*To defat beef broth, skim fat from surface of broth with spoon. Or, place can of broth in refrigerator at least 2 hours ahead of time. Before using, remove fat that has hardened on surface of broth.

1. Spray large saucepan with nonstick cooking spray; heat over medium heat. Add beef; cook and stir until browned on all sides.

2. Stir in broth, potatoes, tomatoes, onion, carrots, barley, vinegar, caraway seeds, marjoram, thyme, salt and pepper; bring to a boil over high heat. Reduce heat to low; cover and simmer 1½ hours. Add green beans; cook, uncovered, 30 minutes or until beef is fork-tender.

Makes 4 servings

Pork and Noodle Soup

1   package (1 ounce) dried shiitake
    mushrooms

4   ounces uncooked thin egg
    noodles

6   cups chicken broth

2   cloves garlic, minced

½   cup shredded carrots

4   ounces ham or Canadian bacon,
    cut into short thin strips

1   tablespoon hoisin sauce

⅛   teaspoon black pepper

2   tablespoons minced fresh chives

1. Place mushrooms in small bowl; cover with warm water. Soak 20 minutes to soften. Drain; squeeze out excess water. Discard stems; slice caps.

2. Meanwhile, cook egg noodles according to package directions until tender. Drain and set aside.

3. Combine broth and garlic in large saucepan; bring to a boil over high heat. Reduce heat to low. Add mushrooms, carrots, ham, hoisin sauce and pepper to saucepan. Simmer 15 minutes. Stir in noodles; simmer until heated through. Sprinkle with chives just before serving.

Makes 6 servings

Pasta Meatball Soup

10 ounces 95% lean ground beef

5 tablespoons uncooked acini di pepe pasta,* divided

¼ cup fresh fine bread crumbs

1 egg

2 tablespoons finely chopped fresh parsley, divided

1 teaspoon dried basil, divided

1 clove garlic, minced

¼ teaspoon salt

⅛ teaspoon black pepper

2 cans (about 14 ounces each) fat-free reduced-sodium beef broth

1 can (about 8 ounces) tomato sauce

⅓ cup chopped onion

Acini di pepe is tiny rice-shaped pasta. Orzo or pastina can be substituted.

1. Combine beef, 2 tablespoons pasta, bread crumbs, egg, 1 tablespoon parsley, ½ teaspoon basil, garlic, salt and pepper in medium bowl. Shape into 28 to 30 (1-inch) meatballs.

2. Bring broth, tomato sauce, onion and remaining ½ teaspoon basil to a boil in large saucepan over medium-high heat. Carefully add meatballs to broth mixture. Reduce heat to medium-low; simmer, covered, 20 minutes.

3. Add remaining 3 tablespoons pasta; cook 10 minutes or until tender. Garnish with remaining 1 tablespoon parsley.

Makes 4 servings

Kansas City Steak Soup

½ pound lean ground beef

3 cups frozen mixed vegetables

2 cups water

1 can (about 14 ounces) stewed tomatoes

1 cup chopped onion

1 cup sliced celery

1 cube beef bouillon

½ to 1 teaspoon black pepper

1 can (about 14 ounces) reduced-sodium beef broth

½ cup all-purpose flour

1. Brown beef in large saucepan over medium-high heat 6 to 8 minutes, stirring to break up meat. Drain fat.

2. Add mixed vegetables, water, tomatoes, onion, celery, bouillon and pepper to saucepan; bring to a boil.

3. Stir broth into flour in small bowl until smooth. Whisk into beef mixture; stir until blended. Bring to a boil. Reduce heat to medium-low; cover and simmer 15 minutes, stirring frequently.

Makes 6 servings

NOTE: If time permits, allow the soup to simmer an additional 30 minutes to allow the flavors to blend.

Veggie Beef Skillet Soup

¾ pound ground beef

1 tablespoon olive oil

2 cups coarsely chopped cabbage

1 cup chopped green bell pepper

2 cups water

1 can (about 14 ounces) stewed tomatoes

1 cup frozen mixed vegetables

⅓ cup ketchup

1 tablespoon beef bouillon granules

2 teaspoons Worcestershire sauce

2 teaspoons balsamic vinegar

⅛ teaspoon red pepper flakes

¼ cup chopped fresh parsley

1. Brown beef in large skillet over medium-high heat 6 to 8 minutes, stirring to break up meat. Drain fat. Transfer to plate.

2. Heat oil in same skillet. Add cabbage and bell pepper; cook and stir 4 minutes or until cabbage is wilted. Add beef, water, tomatoes, mixed vegetables, ketchup, bouillon, Worcestershire sauce, vinegar and red pepper flakes; bring to a boil. Reduce heat; cover and simmer 20 minutes.

3. Remove from heat; let stand 5 minutes. Stir in parsley just before serving.

Makes 4 servings

Classic French Onion Soup

3 tablespoons peanut oil

3 large yellow onions (about
   2 pounds), cut into thin slices

1 cup dry white wine

3 cans (about 14 ounces each) beef
   or chicken broth

½ teaspoon salt

¼ teaspoon white pepper

1 bouquet garni*

1 loaf French bread

4 ounces grated Gruyère cheese

   Sprigs fresh thyme (optional)

*To prepare bouquet garni, tie together
3 sprigs parsley, 2 sprigs thyme and ½ bay
leaf with cotton string or enclose herbs in
square of cheesecloth secured with string.*

1. Heat oil in Dutch oven over medium-high heat until hot. Add onions; cook and stir 15 minutes or until lightly browned. Reduce heat to medium; cook 30 to 45 minutes until onions are deep golden brown, stirring occasionally.

2. Add wine to Dutch oven; cook over high heat 3 to 5 minutes or until liquid is reduced by half. Add broth, salt, pepper and bouquet garni; bring to a boil. Reduce heat to low. Simmer 15 to 20 minutes; remove bouquet garni; discard.

3. Preheat broiler. Toast bread under broiler about 3 minutes per side.

4. Ladle soup into four heatproof bowls; top with bread and cheese. Broil, 4 inches from heat, 2 to 3 minutes or until cheese is bubbly and browned. Serve immediately. Garnish with thyme, if desired.

Makes 4 servings

Beef and Pasta Soup

1 tablespoon vegetable oil

½ pound beef round steak, cut into ½-inch cubes

1 medium onion, chopped

3 cloves garlic, minced

4 cups canned beef broth

1 can (10¾ ounces) tomato purée

2 teaspoons Italian seasoning

2 bay leaves

1 package (9 ounces) frozen Italian green beans

½ cup uncooked orzo or rosamarina (rice-shaped pastas)

Salt

Lemon slices and fresh oregano (optional)

Freshly grated Parmesan cheese (optional)

French bread (optional)

1. Heat oil in 5-quart Dutch oven over medium-high heat; add beef, onion and garlic. Cook and stir until meat is crusty brown and onion is slightly tender.

2. Stir in broth, tomato purée, Italian seasoning and bay leaves. Bring to a boil over high heat. Reduce heat to medium-low; simmer, uncovered, 45 minutes.

3. Add beans and uncooked pasta. Bring to a boil over high heat. Simmer, uncovered, 8 minutes or until beans and pasta are tender, stirring frequently. Season with salt to taste.

4. Remove and discard bay leaves. Ladle soup into bowls. Garnish with lemon slices and oregano. Serve with freshly grated Parmesan cheese and French bread, if desired.

Makes 5 servings

CHICKEN & TURKEY

Spicy Squash & Chicken Soup

1   tablespoon vegetable oil

1   small onion, finely chopped

1   stalk celery, finely chopped

2   cups cubed delicata or butternut squash (about 1 small)

2   cups chicken broth

1   can (about 14 ounces) diced tomatoes with green chiles

1   cup chopped cooked chicken

½   teaspoon ground ginger

¼   teaspoon salt

⅛   teaspoon ground cumin

⅛   teaspoon black pepper

2   teaspoons lime juice

     Sprigs fresh parsley or cilantro (optional)

1. Heat oil in large saucepan over medium heat. Add onion and celery; cook and stir 5 minutes or just until tender. Stir in squash, broth, tomatoes, chicken, ginger, salt, cumin and pepper.

2. Cover; cook over low heat 30 minutes or until squash is tender. Stir in lime juice. Sprinkle with parsley.

Makes 4 servings

TIP: Delicata and butternut are two types of winter squash. Delicata is an elongated, creamy yellow squash with green striations. Butternut is a long, light orange squash. Both have hard skins. To use, cut the squash lengthwise, scoop out the seeds, peel and cut into cubes.

Cream of Chicken and Tortellini Soup

½ of an 8-ounce package dried tortellini with mushrooms and chicken

2 tablespoons butter

1 cup fresh snow peas, cut into 1-inch pieces

2 tablespoons all-purpose flour

3 cups chicken broth, heated

¼ cup half-and-half

1 cup diced cooked chicken breast

1 green onion, chopped

¼ cup grated Parmesan cheese (optional)

1. Cook tortellini according to package directions or until tender. Drain and set aside.

2. Meanwhile, melt butter in large saucepan over medium heat. Add snow peas; cook and stir 3 minutes or until crisp-tender. Stir in flour; cook and stir 1 minute. Stir in broth; cook and stir until mixture is slightly thickened. Stir in half-and-half, chicken, green onion and tortellini. Simmer 2 minutes or until pasta is heated through.

3. Garnish with cheese.

Makes 4 servings

Meatball Soup

¾ pound ground turkey

1 egg white

¼ cup Italian-seasoned dry bread crumbs

3 cloves garlic, minced, divided

3 teaspoons Italian seasoning, divided

¾ teaspoon whole fennel seeds, crushed

½ teaspoon salt

⅛ teaspoon black pepper

¾ cup chopped onion

8 ounces hubbard or other winter yellow squash, peeled, seeded and cut into ¾-inch pieces

3 cans (about 14 ounces each) fat-free reduced-sodium chicken broth

1 can (about 15 ounces) great Northern beans, rinsed and drained

1 can (about 15 ounces) diced tomatoes

1 cup frozen peas

4 ounces uncooked ditalini pasta

Salt and black pepper

Minced fresh parsley

1. Preheat oven to 375°F.

2. Combine turkey, egg white, bread crumbs, 1 clove garlic, 1 teaspoon Italian seasoning, fennel seeds, ½ teaspoon salt and ⅛ teaspoon pepper in medium bowl. Shape turkey mixture into 18 meatballs.

3. Place meatballs in lightly greased baking pan and bake 15 to 20 minutes or until browned and no longer pink in center. Drain on paper towels.

4. Spray large saucepan with nonstick cooking spray; heat over medium heat until hot. Cook and stir onion, squash and remaining 2 cloves garlic about 5 minutes or until onion is tender. Add remaining 2 teaspoons Italian seasoning and cook 1 minute.

5. Add broth, beans, tomatoes and peas; bring to a boil. Reduce heat and simmer, covered, 5 minutes. Add pasta and simmer, uncovered, about 10 minutes or until pasta is tender. Add meatballs during last 5 minutes of cooking time. Season to taste with salt and pepper. Ladle soup into bowls; sprinkle with parsley.

Makes 6 servings

Turkey Noodle Soup

3 pounds turkey thighs, wings and necks

8 cups water

5 carrots, coarsely chopped, divided

1 small onion, quartered

1 teaspoon salt

¼ teaspoon dried thyme leaves

¼ teaspoon dried sage leaves

1 can (about 14 ounces) chicken broth

6 ounces uncooked egg noodles

Chopped fresh parsley

1. Place turkey in Dutch oven. Add water, 2 carrots, onion, salt, thyme and sage. Bring to a boil over high heat; reduce heat to medium-low. Cover; simmer 1 hour.

2. Add broth. Simmer, uncovered, 30 minutes or until turkey is fork-tender. Remove turkey and vegetables from broth; discard vegetables. Remove meat from bones; discard skin and bones. Cut turkey into bite-size pieces.

3. Return broth to a boil over medium heat. Add turkey, remaining 3 carrots and noodles; simmer, uncovered, 10 minutes or until noodles are tender. Adjust seasoning, if desired. Stir in parsley.

Makes about 6 servings

Acorn Squash Soup with Chicken and Red Pepper Meatballs

1 small to medium acorn squash (about ¾ pound)

½ pound ground lean chicken or turkey

1 red bell pepper, seeded and finely chopped

3 tablespoons cholesterol-free egg substitute

1 teaspoon dried parsley flakes

1 teaspoon ground coriander

½ teaspoon black pepper

¼ teaspoon ground cinnamon

3 cups reduced-sodium vegetable broth

2 tablespoons fat-free sour cream (optional)

Ground red pepper (optional)

1. Pierce squash skin with fork. Place in microwaveable dish; microwave on HIGH 8 to 10 minutes or until tender. Cool 10 minutes.

2. Meanwhile, combine chicken, bell pepper, egg substitute, parsley flakes, coriander, black pepper and cinnamon in large bowl, mix lightly. Shape mixture into eight meatballs. Place meatballs in microwavable dish; microwave on HIGH 5 minutes or until cooked through. Set aside to cool.

3. Remove and discard seeds from cooled squash. Scrape squash flesh from shell into large saucepan; mash squash with potato masher. Add broth and meatballs to saucepan; cook over medium-high heat 12 minutes, stirring occasionally. Add additional liquid, if necessary.

4. Garnish each serving with 1 tablespoon sour cream and ground red pepper.

Makes 2 servings

Rustic Country Turkey Soup

1 cup chopped onion

¾ cup sliced carrots

4 ounces sliced mushrooms

1 teaspoon minced garlic

2 cans (about 14 ounces each) reduced-sodium chicken broth

2 ounces uncooked multigrain rotini pasta

1 teaspoon dried thyme or dried parsley

¼ to ½ teaspoon poultry seasoning

⅛ teaspoon red pepper flakes

2 cups chopped cooked turkey breast

2 tablespoons margarine or olive oil

¼ cup chopped fresh parsley

¼ teaspoon salt

1. Heat Dutch oven over medium-high heat. Coat with nonstick cooking spray. Add onion and carrots. Spray vegetables with nonstick cooking spray. Cook 2 minutes, stirring frequently. Add mushrooms. Cook 2 minutes. Add garlic. Cook and stir 30 seconds. Add broth. Bring to a boil.

2. Add pasta, thyme, poultry seasoning and red pepper flakes. Return to a boil. Reduce heat; cover. Simmer 8 minutes or until pasta is tender.

3. Remove from heat. Add turkey, margarine, fresh parsley and salt. Cover. Let stand 5 minutes before serving.

Makes 5 servings

Chicken Tortilla Soup

2 tablespoons canola oil

½ cup finely chopped onion

½ cup finely chopped carrot

2½ cups shredded cooked rotisserie
   chicken

1 cup thick and chunky salsa

4 cups chicken broth

1 tablespoon lime juice

1 avocado, chopped

10 corn tortilla chips, broken into
   thirds

1. Heat oil in large saucepan over high heat. Add onion and carrot; cook and stir
3 minutes or until onion is translucent.

2. Stir in chicken and salsa. Add broth; bring to a boil. Reduce heat to medium-low;
cover and simmer 5 minutes or until carrot is crisp-tender. Remove from heat; stir in lime
juice.

3. Top with avocado and tortilla chips before serving.

Makes 5 servings

Chunky Chicken and Vegetable Soup

1 tablespoon canola oil

1 boneless skinless chicken breast (about ¼ pound), diced

½ cup chopped green bell pepper

½ cup thinly sliced celery

2 green onions, sliced

2 cans (about 14 ounces each) fat-free reduced-sodium chicken broth

1 cup water

½ cup sliced carrots

2 tablespoons reduced-fat whipping cream

⅛ teaspoon black pepper

1 tablespoon finely chopped fresh parsley (optional)

¼ teaspoon dried thyme (optional)

1. Heat oil in large saucepan over medium heat. Add chicken; cook and stir 4 to 5 minutes or until cooked through. Add bell pepper, celery and green onions. Cook and stir 7 minutes or until vegetables are tender.

2. Add broth, water, carrots, cream, black pepper, parsley and thyme, if desired. Simmer 10 minutes or until carrots are tender.

Makes 4 servings

Chicken Curry Soup

6 ounces boneless skinless chicken breasts, cut into ½-inch pieces

3½ teaspoons curry powder, divided

1 teaspoon olive oil

¾ cup chopped apple

½ cup sliced carrot

⅓ cup sliced celery

¼ teaspoon ground cloves

2 cans (about 14 ounces each) fat-free reduced-sodium chicken broth

½ cup orange juice

4 ounces uncooked rotini pasta

Plain fat-free yogurt (optional)

1. Coat chicken with 3 teaspoons curry powder. Heat oil in large saucepan over medium heat until hot. Add chicken; cook and stir 3 minutes or until cooked through. Remove from pan; set aside.

2. Add apple, carrot, celery, remaining ½ teaspoon curry powder and cloves to same saucepan; cook 5 minutes, stirring occasionally. Add broth and orange juice; bring to a boil over high heat.

3. Reduce heat to medium-low. Add pasta; cover. Cook, stirring occasionally, 8 to 10 minutes or until pasta is tender; add chicken. Remove from heat. Ladle into soup tureen or individual bowls. Top each serving with dollop of yogurt, if desired.

Makes 4 servings

Bounty Soup

1 to 2 yellow crookneck squash (about ½ pound)

2 teaspoons vegetable oil

¾ pound boneless skinless chicken breasts, chopped

2 cups frozen mixed vegetables

1 teaspoon dried parsley flakes

⅛ teaspoon salt

⅛ teaspoon dried rosemary

⅛ teaspoon dried thyme

⅛ teaspoon black pepper

1 can (about 14 ounces) fat-free reduced-sodium chicken broth

1 can (about 14 ounces) stewed tomatoes

1. Cut wide part of squash in half lengthwise; lay flat and cut crosswise into ¼-inch-thick slices. Cut narrow part of squash into ¼-inch-thick slices.

2. Heat oil in large saucepan over medium-high heat. Add chicken; stir-fry 2 minutes. Stir in squash, mixed vegetables, parsley, salt, rosemary, thyme and pepper. Add broth and tomatoes, breaking large tomatoes apart. Cover; bring to a boil. Reduce heat to low; cover. Cook 5 minutes or until vegetables are tender. Garnish as desired.

Makes 4 servings

TIP: Yellow squash are also known as summer squash. They have thin, edible skins with a creamy white flesh. Because they are perishable, they should be stored in the refrigerator and used within 5 days of purchase.

Chicken, Barley and Vegetable Soup

½ pound boneless skinless chicken breasts, cut into ½-inch pieces

½ pound boneless skinless chicken thighs, cut into ½-inch pieces

¾ teaspoon salt

¼ teaspoon black pepper

1 tablespoon olive oil

½ cup uncooked pearl barley

4 cans (about 14 ounces each) fat-free reduced-sodium chicken broth

2 cups water

1 bay leaf

2 cups whole baby carrots

2 cups diced peeled potatoes

2 cups sliced mushrooms

2 cups frozen peas

3 tablespoons reduced-fat sour cream

1 tablespoon chopped fresh dill *or* 1 teaspoon dried dill weed

1. Sprinkle chicken with salt and pepper. Heat oil in large saucepan over medium-high heat. Add chicken; cook without stirring 2 minutes or until golden. Turn chicken; cook 2 minutes. Remove chicken to plate.

2. Add barley to saucepan; cook and stir 1 to 2 minutes or until barley starts to brown, adding 1 tablespoon broth if needed to prevent burning. Add remaining broth, water and bay leaf; bring to a boil. Reduce heat to low; cover and simmer 30 minutes.

3. Add chicken, carrots, potatoes and mushrooms; cook 10 minutes or until vegetables are tender. Add peas; cook 2 minutes. Remove and discard bay leaf.

4. Top with sour cream and dill; serve immediately.

Makes 6 servings

Southwest Corn and Turkey Soup

2 dried ancho chiles (each about 4 inches long) *or* 6 dried New Mexico chiles (each about 6 inches long)*

1 medium onion, thinly sliced

3 cloves garlic, minced

1 teaspoon ground cumin

3 cans (about 14 ounces each) fat-free reduced-sodium chicken broth

2 small zucchini, cut into ½-inch slices

1½ to 2 cups shredded cooked turkey

1 can (about 15 ounces) black beans or chickpeas, rinsed and drained

1 package (10 ounces) frozen corn

¼ cup yellow cornmeal

1 teaspoon dried oregano

⅓ cup chopped fresh cilantro

Chile peppers can sting and irritate the skin, so wear rubber gloves when handling peppers and do not touch your eyes.

1. Cut stems from chiles; remove and discard seeds. Place chiles in medium bowl; cover with boiling water. Let stand 20 to 40 minutes or until chiles are softened; drain. Cut open lengthwise and lay flat on work surface. Scrape chile pulp from skin with edge of small knife. Finely mince pulp; set aside.

2. Spray large saucepan with nonstick cooking spray; heat over medium heat. Add onion; cook and stir 3 to 4 minutes. Add garlic and cumin; cook and stir 30 seconds. Stir in broth, reserved chile pulp, zucchini, turkey, beans, corn, cornmeal and oregano; bring to a boil over high heat. Reduce heat to low; simmer 15 minutes or until zucchini is tender.

3. Stir in cilantro just before serving.

Makes 6 servings

Skillet Chicken Soup

1 teaspoon paprika

½ teaspoon salt

¼ teaspoon black pepper

¾ pound boneless skinless chicken breasts or thighs, cut into ¾-inch pieces

2 teaspoons vegetable oil

1 large onion, chopped

1 red bell pepper, cut into ½-inch pieces

3 cloves garlic, minced

3 cups fat-free reduced-sodium chicken broth

1 can (19 ounces) reduced-sodium cannellini beans or small white beans, rinsed and drained

3 cups sliced savoy or napa cabbage

½ cup fat-free herb-flavored croutons, slightly crushed (optional)

1. Combine paprika, salt and black pepper in medium bowl; stir to blend. Add chicken; toss to coat.

2. Heat oil in large deep nonstick skillet over medium-high heat. Add chicken, onion, bell pepper and garlic; cook and stir 8 minutes or until chicken is cooked through.

3. Add broth and beans; bring to a simmer. Cover and simmer 5 minutes. Stir in cabbage; cover and simmer 3 minutes or until cabbage is wilted. Ladle into six shallow bowls; top evenly with crushed croutons, if desired.

Makes 6 servings

TIP: Savoy cabbage, also called curly cabbage, is round with pale green crinkled leaves. Napa cabbage is also known as Chinese cabbage and is elongated with light green stalks.

Turkey Vegetable Rice Soup

1½ pounds turkey drumsticks (2 small)

8 cups cold water

1 medium onion, cut into quarters

2 tablespoons soy sauce

¼ teaspoon black pepper

1 bay leaf

2 carrots, sliced

⅓ cup uncooked rice

4 ounces mushrooms, sliced

1 cup fresh snow peas, cut in half crosswise

1 cup coarsely chopped bok choy

1. Place turkey in 5-quart Dutch oven. Add water, onion, soy sauce, pepper and bay leaf. Bring to a boil over high heat. Reduce heat to medium-low; simmer, uncovered, 1½ hours or until turkey is tender.

2. Remove turkey from Dutch oven; let broth cool slightly. Skim fat. Remove and discard bay leaf.

3. Remove turkey meat from bones; discard skin and bones. Cut turkey into bite-size pieces.

4. Add carrots and rice to Dutch oven. Bring to a boil over high heat. Reduce heat to medium-low; simmer, uncovered, 10 minutes.

5. Add mushrooms and turkey to soup. Bring to a boil over high heat. Reduce heat to medium-low; simmer, uncovered, 5 minutes.

6. Stir snow peas and bok choy into soup. Bring to a boil over high heat. Reduce heat to medium-low; simmer, uncovered, 8 minutes or until rice and vegetables are tender.

Makes 6 servings

Chicken Enchilada Soup

2 tablespoons vegetable oil, divided

1½ pounds boneless skinless chicken breasts, cut into ½-inch cubes

½ cup chopped onion

2 cloves garlic, minced

2 cans (about 14 ounces each) chicken broth

3 cups water, divided

1 cup masa harina

1 package (16 ounces) pasteurized process cheese product, cubed

1 can (10 ounces) mild red enchilada sauce

1 teaspoon chili powder

½ teaspoon salt

½ teaspoon ground cumin

Chopped fresh tomatoes

Crispy tortilla strips*

*If tortilla strips are not available, crumble tortilla chips into bite-size pieces.

1. Heat 1 tablespoon oil in large saucepan or Dutch oven over medium-high heat. Add chicken; cook and stir 10 minutes or until no longer pink. Transfer chicken to large bowl with slotted spoon; drain fat from saucepan.

2. Heat remaining 1 tablespoon oil in same saucepan over medium-high heat. Add onion and garlic; cook and stir 3 minutes or until softened. Stir in broth.

3. Whisk 2 cups water into masa harina in large bowl until smooth. Whisk mixture into broth in saucepan. Stir in cheese product, remaining 1 cup water, enchilada sauce, chili powder, salt and cumin; bring to a boil over high heat. Add chicken. Reduce heat to medium-low; cook 30 minutes, stirring frequently. Ladle soup into bowls; top with tomatoes and tortilla strips.

Makes 8 to 10 servings

Chicken and Gnocchi Soup

¼ cup (½ stick) butter

1 tablespoon extra virgin olive oil

1 cup finely diced onion

2 stalks celery, finely chopped

2 cloves garlic, minced

¼ cup all-purpose flour

4 cups half-and-half

1 can (about 14 ounces) chicken broth

1 teaspoon salt

½ teaspoon dried thyme

½ teaspoon dried parsley flakes

¼ teaspoon ground nutmeg

1 package (about 16 ounces) gnocchi

1 package (6 ounces) fully cooked chicken strips, chopped *or* 1 cup diced cooked chicken

1 cup shredded carrots

1 cup coarsely chopped fresh spinach

1. Melt butter in large saucepan or Dutch oven over medium heat; add oil. Add onion, celery and garlic; cook about 10 minutes or until vegetables are softened and onion is translucent, stirring occasionally.

2. Whisk in flour; cook and stir about 1 minute. Whisk in half-and-half; cook about 15 minutes or until thickened.

3. Whisk in broth, salt, thyme, parsley and nutmeg; cook 10 minutes or until slightly thickened. Add gnocchi, chicken, carrots and spinach; cook about 5 minutes or until gnocchi is heated through.

Makes 6 to 8 servings

Chicken Noodle Soup

2 tablespoons butter

1 cup chopped onion

1 cup sliced carrots

½ cup diced celery

2 tablespoons vegetable oil

1 pound chicken breast tenderloins

1 pound chicken thigh fillets

4 cups chicken broth, divided

2 cups water

1 tablespoon minced fresh parsley, plus additional for garnish

1½ teaspoons salt

½ teaspoon black pepper

3 cups uncooked egg noodles

1. Melt butter in large saucepan or Dutch oven over medium-low heat. Add onion, carrots and celery; cook 15 minutes or until vegetables are soft, stirring occasionally.

2. Meanwhile, heat oil in large skillet over medium-high heat. Add chicken in single layer; cook about 12 minutes or until lightly browned and cooked through, turning once. Transfer chicken to cutting board. Add 1 cup broth to skillet; cook 1 minute, scraping up any browned bits from bottom of skillet. Add broth to vegetables. Stir in remaining 3 cups broth, water, 1 tablespoon parsley, salt and pepper.

3. Chop chicken into 1-inch pieces when cool enough to handle. Add to soup; bring to a boil over medium-high heat. Reduce heat to medium-low; cook 15 minutes. Add noodles; cook 15 minutes or until noodles are tender. Ladle soup into bowls; garnish with additional parsley.

Makes 8 servings

Peppery Sicilian Chicken Soup

2 tablespoons olive oil

1 onion, chopped

1 green bell pepper, chopped

3 stalks celery, chopped

3 carrots, chopped

3 cloves garlic, minced

1 tablespoon salt

3 containers (32 ounces each) chicken broth

2 pounds boneless skinless chicken breasts

1 can (28 ounces) diced tomatoes

2 baking potatoes, peeled and cut into ¼-inch pieces

1½ teaspoons ground white pepper*

1½ teaspoons ground black pepper*

½ cup chopped fresh parsley

8 ounces uncooked ditalini pasta

Or substitute additional black pepper for the white pepper.

1. Heat oil in large saucepan or Dutch oven over medium heat. Stir in onion, bell pepper, celery and carrots. Reduce heat to medium-low; cover and cook 10 to 15 minutes or until vegetables are tender but not browned, stirring occasionally. Stir in garlic and salt; cover and cook 5 minutes.

2. Add broth, chicken, tomatoes, potatoes, white pepper and black pepper; bring to a boil. Reduce heat to low; cover and cook 1 hour. Remove chicken; cool slightly. Shred chicken and return to saucepan with parsley.

3. Meanwhile, cook pasta in large saucepan of boiling salted water 7 minutes (or 1 minute less than package directs for al dente). Drain and add to soup. Taste and add additional salt, if desired.

Makes 8 to 10 servings

Shortcut Chicken Tortilla Soup

2   cans (about 14 ounces each) reduced-sodium chicken broth

4   boneless skinless chicken breasts (about 1 pound)

2   jars (16 ounces each) corn and black bean salsa

3   tablespoons vegetable oil

1   tablespoon taco seasoning mix

1   package (3 ounces) ramen noodles, any flavor, broken into small pieces*

4   ounces Monterey Jack cheese, grated

Discard seasoning packet.

1. Bring broth to a simmer in large saucepan. Add chicken; cook 12 to 15 minutes or until no longer pink in center. Remove chicken to cutting board; set aside until cool enough to handle. Shred chicken with two forks.

2. Add salsa to saucepan; cook 5 minutes or until soup comes to a simmer. Return shredded chicken to saucepan; cook 5 minutes until thoroughly heated.

3. Combine oil and taco seasoning in small bowl. Add noodles; toss to coat. Cook and stir noodles in medium skillet over medium heat 8 to 10 minutes or until toasted. Top soup with toasted noodles and grated cheese.

Makes 6 servings

TIP: Serve soup with lime wedges, chopped avocado or fresh cilantro on the side—top with your favorites!

Chicken and Homemade Noodle Soup

¾ cup all-purpose flour

2 teaspoons finely chopped fresh thyme *or* ½ teaspoon dried thyme, divided

¼ teaspoon salt

1 egg yolk, beaten

2 cups plus 3 tablespoons cold water, divided

1 pound boneless skinless chicken thighs, cut into ½- to ¾-inch pieces

5 cups chicken broth

1 onion, chopped

1 carrot, thinly sliced

¾ cup frozen peas

Chopped fresh Italian parsley

1. For noodles, combine flour, 1 teaspoon thyme and salt in small bowl. Stir in egg yolk and 3 tablespoons water until well blended. Shape into a small ball. Place dough on lightly floured surface; flatten slightly. Knead 5 minutes or until dough is smooth and elastic, adding more flour to prevent sticking, if necessary. Cover with plastic wrap. Let stand 15 minutes.

2. Roll out dough to ⅛-inch thickness or thinner on lightly floured surface. If dough is too elastic, let rest several minutes. Let dough rest about 30 minutes to dry slightly. Cut into ¼-inch-wide strips. Cut strips 1½ to 2 inches long; set aside.

3. Combine chicken and remaining 2 cups water in medium saucepan. Bring to a boil over high heat. Reduce heat to medium-low; cover and simmer 5 minutes or until chicken is cooked through. Drain chicken.

4. Combine broth, onion, carrot and remaining 1 teaspoon thyme in Dutch oven or large saucepan. Bring to a boil over high heat. Add noodles. Reduce heat to medium-low; simmer, uncovered, 8 minutes or until noodles are tender. Stir in chicken and peas; bring to a boil. Sprinkle with parsley.

Makes 4 servings

FISH & SHELLFISH

"Dearhearts" Seafood Bisque

2 tablespoons olive oil

1 onion, finely chopped

2 cups chicken broth

1 package (9 ounces) frozen artichoke hearts, thawed

½ cup dry white wine

1 pound mixed shellfish (raw shrimp, peeled and deveined; raw scallops; and/or canned crabmeat)

1 cup whipping cream

2 tablespoons chopped fresh parsley

1 teaspoon salt

½ teaspoon ground nutmeg

¼ teaspoon white pepper

1. Heat oil in large saucepan over medium-high heat. Add onion; cook and stir 5 minutes or until softened. Add broth, artichokes and wine; bring to a boil over medium-high heat. Reduce heat to low; cover and simmer 5 to 7 minutes.

2. Working in batches, process soup in food processor or blender until smooth. Return soup to saucepan.

3. Stir in shellfish, cream, parsley, salt, nutmeg and pepper; bring to a simmer over medium heat. Reduce heat to low; simmer, uncovered, 5 to 10 minutes. **Do not boil.** (Shellfish will become tough if soup boils.)

Makes 6 servings

Corn and Crab Gazpacho

1 cucumber, peeled, seeded and coarsely chopped

3 green onions, coarsely chopped

2 tablespoons coarsely chopped fresh Italian parsley or cilantro

2 pounds grape or cherry tomatoes

1 cup cooked fresh corn (1 large ear) *or* 1 cup thawed frozen corn

3 cups tomato juice, chilled

3 tablespoons olive oil

2 tablespoons red wine vinegar

1¼ teaspoons red pepper flakes

1 teaspoon salt

¼ teaspoon black pepper

1½ cups flaked cooked crabmeat (about 8 ounces) *or* 8 ounces cooked baby shrimp

1. Combine cucumber, green onions and parsley in food processor. Process using on/off pulsing action until finely chopped. Transfer to large pitcher or bowl. Add tomatoes to food processor. Process using on/off pulsing action until finely chopped. Add to cucumber mixture.

2. Stir corn into pitcher. Add tomato juice, oil, vinegar, red pepper flakes, salt and black pepper. Stir well. Cover; refrigerate 1 to 3 hours.

3. Pour gazpacho into 6 bowls. Top each serving with ¼ cup crabmeat.

Makes 6 servings

VARIATION: For a vegetarian version, omit crab.

NOTE: Gazpacho can be made several hours in advance and chilled. Bring to room temperature before serving.

New England Fish Chowder

¼ pound bacon, diced

1 cup chopped onion

½ cup chopped celery

2 cups diced peeled russet potatoes

2 tablespoons all-purpose flour

2 cups water

1 teaspoon salt

1 bay leaf

1 teaspoon dried dill weed

½ teaspoon dried thyme

½ teaspoon black pepper

1 pound cod, haddock or halibut fillets, skinned, boned and cut into 1-inch pieces

2 cups milk or half-and-half

1. Cook bacon in large saucepan or Dutch oven over medium-high heat, stirring occasionally. Drain on paper towels.

2. Add onion and celery to drippings in saucepan; cook and stir until onion is soft. Add potatoes; cook and stir 1 minute. Add flour; cook and stir 1 minute. Add water, salt, bay leaf, dill weed, thyme and pepper; bring to a boil over high heat. Reduce heat to low; cover and simmer 25 minutes or until potatoes are fork-tender.

3. Add fish to saucepan; cover and simmer 5 minutes or until fish begins to flake when tested with fork. Remove and discard bay leaf. Stir in bacon. Add milk; cook and stir until heated through. **Do not boil.**

Makes 4 to 6 servings

New Orleans Fish Soup

1 can (about 15 ounces) cannellini beans, rinsed and drained

1 can (about 14 ounces) reduced-sodium chicken broth

1 yellow squash, halved lengthwise and sliced (1 cup)

1 tablespoon Cajun seasoning

2 cans (about 14 ounces each) no-salt-added stewed tomatoes

1 pound skinless firm fish fillets, such as grouper, cod or haddock, cut into 1-inch pieces

½ cup sliced green onions

1 teaspoon grated orange peel

1. Combine beans, broth, squash and Cajun seasoning in large saucepan; bring to a boil over high heat. Reduce heat to medium-low.

2. Stir in tomatoes and fish; cover and simmer 3 to 5 minutes or until fish begins to flake when tested with fork. Stir in green onions and orange peel.

Makes 4 servings

Cod Chowder

2 tablespoons vegetable oil

1 pound unpeeled red potatoes, diced

2 medium leeks, halved and thinly sliced

2 stalks celery, diced

1 bulb fennel, diced

½ yellow or red bell pepper, diced

2 teaspoons chopped fresh thyme

¾ teaspoon salt

½ to ¾ teaspoon black pepper

2 tablespoons all-purpose flour

2 cups clam juice

1 cup water

1 cup half-and-half

1½ pounds cod, cut into 1-inch pieces

1 cup frozen corn

¼ cup finely chopped fresh Italian parsley

1. Heat oil in Dutch oven or large saucepan over medium heat. Add potatoes, leeks, celery, fennel, bell pepper, thyme, salt and black pepper; cover and cook about 8 minutes or until vegetables are slightly softened, stirring occasionally. Add flour; cook and stir 1 minute.

2. Stir in clam juice and water; bring to a boil over high heat. Reduce heat to medium-low; cover and simmer about 10 minutes or until potatoes are tender. Remove from heat.

3. Transfer 1½ cups soup to blender; add half-and-half; blend until smooth.

4. Add cod, corn and parsley to saucepan; bring to a simmer over medium-high heat. Stir in blended soup mixture; cover and cook over medium heat about 3 minutes or until fish is firm and opaque, stirring occasionally. Serve immediately.

Makes 6 to 8 servings

Tortilla Soup with Grouper

1	tablespoon vegetable oil		1	teaspoon ground cumin
1	onion, chopped		1	teaspoon chili powder
2	cloves garlic, minced		1	teaspoon salt
3½	cups chicken broth		⅛	teaspoon black pepper
1½	cups tomato juice		3	corn tortillas, cut into 1-inch strips
1	cup chopped tomatoes		1	cup corn
1	can (4 ounces) diced green chiles, drained		1	pound grouper fillets, cut into 1-inch pieces
2	teaspoons Worcestershire sauce			

1. Heat oil in large saucepan over medium-high heat. Add onion and garlic; cook and stir until softened. Stir in broth, tomato juice, tomatoes, chiles, Worcestershire sauce, cumin, chili powder, salt and pepper; bring to a boil. Reduce heat to medium-low; cover and simmer 10 minutes.

2. Add tortillas and corn; cover and simmer 8 to 10 minutes.

3. Stir in grouper; simmer, uncovered, until fish begins to flake when tested with fork.

Makes 6 servings

Salmon and Wild Rice Chowder

1   teaspoon margarine

1   red onion, chopped

1   red bell pepper, chopped

1   cup fresh or frozen green beans,
    cut into 1-inch pieces

1½ teaspoons minced fresh dill

1   teaspoon salt

⅛   teaspoon black pepper

3   cups fat-free vegetable broth

1   cup cooked wild rice

12 ounces skinless salmon filet, cut
    into 1-inch pieces

2   teaspoons all-purpose flour

½   cup fat-free half-and-half

1. Melt margarine in large saucepan over high heat. Add onion, bell pepper and green beans; cook and stir 5 minutes. Stir in dill, salt and black pepper. Pour in broth; bring to a simmer.

2. Add wild rice and salmon to saucepan. Reduce heat to low; cover and simmer 6 to 8 minutes or until salmon flakes easily when tested with fork.

3. Place flour in small bowl. Slowly whisk in half-and-half. Stir into saucepan. Cook until heated through.

Makes 8 servings

Italian Fish Soup

1 cup meatless pasta sauce

¾ cup fat-free reduced-sodium chicken broth

¾ cup water

1 teaspoon Italian seasoning

¾ cup uncooked small pasta shells

4 ounces fresh halibut or haddock steak, 1 inch thick, skinned and cut into 1-inch pieces

1½ cups frozen vegetable blend, such as broccoli, carrots and water chestnuts *or* broccoli, carrots and cauliflower

1. Combine pasta sauce, broth, water and Italian seasoning in medium saucepan; bring to a boil over high heat. Stir in pasta; return to a boil. Reduce heat to medium-low; cover and simmer 5 minutes.

2. Stir in fish and frozen vegetables; return to a boil. Reduce heat to medium-low; cover and simmer 4 to 5 minutes or until pasta is tender and fish begins to flake when tested with fork.

Makes 2 servings

Savory Seafood Soup

2½ cups water or chicken broth

1½ cups dry white wine

1 onion, chopped

½ red bell pepper, chopped

½ green bell pepper, chopped

1 clove garlic, minced

½ pound halibut, cut into 1-inch pieces

½ pound sea scallops, cut into halves

1 teaspoon dried thyme

Juice of ½ lime

Dash hot pepper sauce

Salt and black pepper

1. Combine water, wine, onion, bell peppers and garlic in large saucepan; bring to a boil over high heat. Reduce heat to medium-low; cover and simmer 15 minutes or until bell peppers are tender, stirring occasionally.

2. Add fish, scallops and thyme; cook 2 minutes or until fish and scallops turn opaque. Stir in lime juice and hot pepper sauce. Season with salt and black pepper.

Makes 4 servings

TIP: Halibut is considered a lean fish because it has a low fat content. If halibut is not available, cod, ocean perch or haddock can be substituted. When buying fresh fish, store it tightly wrapped in the refrigerator and plan on using it within 2 days of purchase.

Creamy Crab Chowder

1 tablespoon butter

1 cup finely chopped onion

2 cloves garlic, minced

1 cup finely chopped celery

½ cup finely chopped green bell pepper

½ cup finely chopped red bell pepper

3 cans (about 14 ounces each) chicken broth

3 cups diced peeled potatoes

1 package (10 ounces) frozen corn

2 cans (6½ ounces each) lump crabmeat

½ cup half-and-half

¼ teaspoon black pepper

1. Melt butter in large saucepan or Dutch oven over medium heat. Add onion and garlic; cook and stir 6 minutes or until softened but not browned. Add celery and bell peppers; cook 8 minutes or until celery is tender, stirring frequently.

2. Stir in broth and potatoes; bring to a boil over high heat. Reduce heat to low; simmer 10 minutes. Add corn; cook 5 minutes or until potatoes are tender.

3. Drain crabmeat; place in small bowl. Flake to break up large pieces; add to saucepan. Stir in half-and-half and black pepper; bring to a simmer. *Do not boil.*

Makes 6 to 8 servings

Scallops & Mock Seaweed Soup

4   ounces fresh spinach, washed

3   carrots, peeled

6   cups chicken broth

4   green onions, sliced

2   tablespoons chopped fresh dill

2   teaspoons white wine
     Worcestershire sauce

2   teaspoons lemon juice

1   pound bay scallops, rinsed and
     patted dry

Salt and white pepper to taste

1. To cut spinach into chiffonade strips, make "V-shaped" cut at stem end. Roll up leaf jelly-roll fashion. Slice crosswise into ½-inch-thick slices with chef's knife. Repeat with remaining leaves; set aside.

2. To cut carrot decoratively, use citrus stripper or grapefruit spoon to cut groove into carrot, cutting lengthwise from stem end to tip. Continue to cut grooves around carrot about ¼ inch apart until completely around carrot. Thinly slice crosswise. Repeat with remaining carrots.

3. Bring broth to a simmer in large saucepan; add carrot slices. Bring to a boil; simmer 5 minutes or until carrots are crisp-tender.

4. Add spinach, green onions, dill, Worcestershire sauce and lemon juice to soup; simmer 1 to 2 minutes.

5. Add scallops; simmer briefly until scallops turn opaque. Season with salt and pepper; serve immediately.

Makes 6 servings

Salmon, Corn & Barley Chowder

1 teaspoon canola oil

¼ cup chopped onion

1 clove garlic, minced

2½ cups fat-free reduced-sodium chicken broth

¼ cup quick-cooking barley

1 tablespoon water

1 tablespoon all-purpose flour

1 can (4 ounces) salmon, drained

1 cup frozen corn, thawed

⅓ cup reduced-fat (2%) milk

½ teaspoon chili powder

¼ teaspoon ground cumin

¼ teaspoon dried oregano

⅛ teaspoon salt

1 tablespoon minced fresh cilantro

⅛ teaspoon black pepper

Lime wedges (optional)

1. Heat oil in medium saucepan over medium heat until hot. Add onion and garlic. Cook and stir 1 to 2 minutes or until onion is tender.

2. Add broth; bring to a boil. Stir in barley. Cover; reduce heat and simmer 10 minutes or until barley is tender.

3. Stir water gradually into flour in small bowl until smooth; set aside. Remove and discard bones and skin from salmon; flake into bite-size pieces.

4. Add salmon, corn and milk to saucepan; stir until blended. Stir in flour paste, chili powder, cumin, oregano and salt. Simmer gently 2 to 3 minutes or until slightly thickened. Stir in cilantro and pepper. Serve with lime wedges, if desired.

Makes 2 servings

VEGETABLES & BEANS

Black Bean Soup

2 tablespoons vegetable oil

1 cup diced onion

1 stalk celery, diced

2 carrots, diced

½ small green bell pepper, diced

4 cloves garlic, minced

4 cans (about 15 ounces each) black beans, rinsed and drained, divided

4 cups (32 ounces) chicken or vegetable broth, divided

2 tablespoons cider vinegar

2 teaspoons chili powder

½ teaspoon salt

½ teaspoon ground red pepper

½ teaspoon ground cumin

¼ teaspoon liquid smoke

Garnishes: sour cream, chopped green onions and shredded Cheddar cheese

1. Heat oil in large saucepan or Dutch oven over medium-low heat. Add onion, celery, carrots, bell pepper and garlic; cook 10 minutes, stirring occasionally.

2. Combine half of beans and 1 cup broth in food processor or blender; process until smooth. Add to vegetables in saucepan.

3. Stir in remaining beans, remaining broth, vinegar, chili powder, salt, red pepper, cumin and liquid smoke; bring to a boil over high heat. Reduce heat to medium-low; cook 1 hour or until vegetables are tender and soup is thickened. Garnish as desired.

Makes 4 to 6 servings

White Bean and Escarole Soup

1½ cups dried baby lima beans, rinsed and sorted

1 teaspoon olive oil

½ cup chopped celery

⅓ cup coarsely chopped onion

2 cloves garlic, minced

2 cans (about 14 ounces each) no-salt-added whole tomatoes, undrained and chopped

½ cup chopped fresh parsley

2 tablespoons chopped fresh rosemary

¼ teaspoon black pepper

3 cups shredded fresh escarole

1. Place dried lima beans in large glass bowl; cover completely with water. Soak 6 to 8 hours or overnight. Drain beans; place in large saucepan or Dutch oven. Cover beans with about 3 cups water; bring to a boil over high heat. Reduce heat to low. Cover and simmer about 1 hour or until soft. Drain; set aside.

2. Heat oil in small skillet over medium heat. Add celery, onion and garlic; cook and stir 5 minutes or until onion is tender. Remove from heat.

3. Add celery mixture and tomatoes to beans. Stir in parsley, rosemary and pepper. Simmer, covered, over low heat 15 minutes. Add escarole; simmer 5 minutes.

Makes 6 servings

TIP: Store dried lima beans (also known as butter beans) in an airtight container in a cool, dry place for up to 1 year. When soaking, do not allow beans to soak for longer than 12 hours or they may start to ferment.

Butternut Squash Soup

2 teaspoons olive oil

1 large sweet onion, chopped

1 medium red bell pepper, chopped

2 packages (10 ounces each) frozen puréed butternut squash, thawed

1 can (10¾ ounces) condensed reduced-sodium chicken broth, undiluted

¼ teaspoon ground nutmeg

⅛ teaspoon black pepper

½ cup fat-free half-and-half

1. Heat oil in large saucepan over medium-high heat. Add onion and bell pepper; cook 5 minutes, stirring occasionally. Add squash, broth, nutmeg and black pepper; bring to a boil over high heat. Reduce heat; cover and simmer 15 minutes or until vegetables are very tender.

2. Purée soup in saucepan with hand-held immersion blender or in batches in food processor or blender. Return soup to saucepan.

3. Stir in half-and-half; heat through. Add additional half-and-half, if necessary, to thin soup to desired consistency.

Makes 4 servings

SERVING SUGGESTION: Garnish with a swirl of fat-free half-and-half or a sprinkling of fresh parsley.

TIP: Butternut squash is a type of winter squash and is an excellent source of beta-carotene. It's also a very good source of vitamin C, potassium and dietary fiber.

Country Bean Soup

1¼ cups dried navy beans or lima beans, rinsed and sorted

2½ cups water

4 ounces ham or salt pork, chopped

¼ cup chopped onion

½ teaspoon dried oregano

¼ teaspoon salt

¼ teaspoon ground ginger

¼ teaspoon dried sage

¼ teaspoon black pepper

2 cups milk

2 tablespoons butter

1. Place beans in large saucepan; add water to cover. Bring to a boil over medium-high heat. Reduce heat to medium-low; simmer 2 minutes. Remove from heat; cover and let stand 1 hour.

2. Drain beans and return to saucepan. Stir in 2½ cups water, ham, onion, oregano, salt, ginger, sage and pepper. Bring to a boil over high heat. Reduce heat to medium-low; cover and simmer 2 hours or until beans are tender. (If necessary, add additional water to keep beans covered during cooking.)

3. Add milk and butter; cook and stir until heated through.

Makes 6 servings

Mushroom Barley Soup

2 tablespoons butter

8 ounces sliced mushrooms

½ cup chopped onion

½ cup chopped carrots

1 clove garlic, minced

1 teaspoon dried thyme

¼ teaspoon black pepper

¼ cup dry white wine

4 cups chicken broth

¾ cup quick-cooking barley

1. Heat butter in large saucepan over medium-high heat. Add mushrooms, onion, carrots, garlic, thyme and pepper; cook and stir 6 to 8 minutes or until mushrooms begin to brown. Add wine, stirring to scrape up browned bits.

2. Stir in broth; bring to a boil over high heat. Stir in barley. Reduce heat to low; simmer, partially covered, 15 minutes or until barley is tender.

Makes about 4 servings

TIPS: For extra flavor, use a mix of button and baby bella mushrooms. For a vegetarian soup, substitute vegetable broth for the chicken broth.

Chilled Cucumber Soup

1 large cucumber, peeled, seeded and coarsely chopped

¾ cup plain nonfat Greek yogurt

¼ cup packed fresh dill

½ teaspoon salt (optional)

⅛ teaspoon ground white pepper (optional)

1½ cups fat-free reduced-sodium chicken or vegetable broth

4 sprigs fresh dill

1. Place cucumber in blender or food processor; process until finely chopped. Add yogurt, ¼ cup dill, salt and pepper, if desired; process until smooth.

2. Transfer mixture to large bowl; stir in broth. Cover and refrigerate at least 2 hours or up to 24 hours. Ladle into bowls; garnish with dill sprigs.

Makes 4 servings

Winter Squash Soup

1 tablespoon low-fat vegetable oil spread

1 tablespoon minced shallot or onion

2 cloves garlic, minced

3 sprigs fresh thyme

Pinch dried rosemary

2 packages (10 ounces each) frozen butternut squash, thawed

1 cup fat-free reduced-sodium chicken broth

3 tablespoons fat-free (skim) milk

Fat-free sour cream (optional)

1. Melt vegetable oil spread in medium saucepan over medium heat. Add shallot, garlic, thyme and rosemary; cook and stir 2 to 3 minutes or until shallot is tender. Add squash and broth; bring to a boil. Add milk; stir until blended.

2. Remove and discard thyme. Working in batches, process soup in blender or food processor until smooth. (Add additional broth or water to make soup thinner, if desired.) Top each serving with dollop of sour cream, if desired.

Makes 4 servings

French Onion Soup for Deux

2 teaspoons olive oil

¾ pound yellow onions, halved lengthwise and cut into thin strips

1 clove garlic, thinly sliced

⅛ teaspoon salt

¼ teaspoon black pepper

1 cup fat-free reduced-sodium chicken broth

1 cup water

1 tablespoon balsamic vinegar

1 bay leaf

½ teaspoon dried thyme

2 thick slices crusty, peasant-style, whole wheat bread

¼ cup (1 ounce) shredded reduced-fat white cheese, such as Muenster or Monterey-Jack

1. Heat oil in large saucepan over medium heat. Add onions and garlic. Cook, stirring frequently, 20 minutes until onions are soft and golden brown. If onions start to stick or burn, reduce heat slightly and add water 1 tablespoon at a time. Sprinkle onions with salt and pepper.

2. Reduce heat to low; add broth, water, vinegar, bay leaf and thyme. Simmer until heated through. Remove and discard bay leaf.

3. Preheat broiler. Toast bread under broiler on both sides. To serve, ladle soup into two ovenproof bowls; top each with toasted bread. Sprinkle bread with cheese. Place bowls on baking sheet. Broil until cheese melts and is bubbly and browned.

Makes 2 servings

Italian Skillet Roasted Vegetable Soup

2 tablespoons olive oil, divided

1 medium orange, red or yellow bell pepper, chopped

1 clove garlic, minced

2 cups water

1 can (about 14 ounces) diced tomatoes

1 medium zucchini, thinly sliced lengthwise

⅛ teaspoon red pepper flakes

1 can (about 15 ounces) navy beans, rinsed and drained

3 to 4 tablespoons chopped fresh basil

1 tablespoon balsamic vinegar

¾ teaspoon salt

½ teaspoon liquid smoke (optional)

1. Heat 1 tablespoon oil in Dutch oven over medium-high heat. Add bell pepper; cook and stir 4 minutes or until edges are browned. Add garlic; cook and stir 15 seconds. Add water, tomatoes, zucchini and red pepper flakes; bring to a boil over high heat. Reduce heat to low; cover and simmer 20 minutes.

2. Add beans, basil, remaining 1 tablespoon oil, vinegar, salt and liquid smoke, if desired; simmer 5 minutes. Remove from heat; let stand, covered, 10 minutes before serving.

Makes 5 servings

Broccoli Cream Soup with Green Onions

1 tablespoon olive oil

2 cups chopped onions

1 pound fresh or frozen broccoli florets or spears

2 cups reduced-sodium chicken or vegetable broth

6 tablespoons reduced-fat cream cheese

1 cup fat-free (skim) milk

¾ teaspoon salt (optional)

⅛ teaspoon ground red pepper

⅓ cup finely chopped green onions

1. Heat oil in large saucepan over medium-high heat. Add onions; cook and stir 4 minutes or until translucent. Add broccoli and broth; bring to a boil. Reduce heat to medium-low; cover and simmer 10 minutes or until broccoli is tender.

2. Working in batches, process mixture in food processor or blender until smooth.* Return mixture to saucepan; heat over medium heat.

3. Whisk in cream cheese until melted. Stir in milk, salt, if desired, and red pepper; cook 2 minutes or until heated through. Top with green onions.

Or, use hand-held immersion blender.

Makes 5 servings

Deep Bayou Chowder

1 tablespoon olive oil

1½ cups chopped onions

1 large green bell pepper, chopped

1 large carrot, chopped

8 ounces red potatoes, diced

1 cup frozen corn

1 cup water

½ teaspoon dried thyme

2 cups milk

2 tablespoons chopped fresh parsley

1½ teaspoons seafood seasoning

¾ teaspoon salt

1. Heat oil in Dutch oven over medium-high heat. Add onions, bell pepper and carrot; cook and stir 4 minutes or until onions are translucent.

2. Add potatoes, corn, water and thyme; bring to a boil over high heat. Reduce heat; cover and simmer 15 minutes or until potatoes are tender. Stir in milk, parsley, seafood seasoning and salt; cook 5 minutes.

Makes 6 servings

Vegetable Lentil Soup with Cilantro

2 medium carrots, thinly sliced

½ cup chopped onion

4 cups water

¾ cup dried lentils, rinsed and sorted

2 teaspoons chicken bouillon or vegetarian chicken-flavored bouillon

½ teaspoon ground cumin

⅛ teaspoon ground red pepper

1 medium tomato, seeded and diced

½ cup chopped roasted red bell peppers

2 teaspoons olive oil

¼ teaspoon salt (optional)

2 tablespoons chopped fresh cilantro

1. Heat large saucepan or Dutch oven over medium-high heat; spray with nonstick cooking spray. Add carrots and onion; cook and stir 4 minutes or until onion is translucent.

2. Add water, lentils, bouillon, cumin and red pepper. Bring to a boil over high heat. Reduce heat; cover and simmer 45 minutes or until lentils are very tender.

3. Remove from heat; stir in tomato, peppers, oil and salt, if desired. Cover and let stand 5 minutes before serving. Garnish with cilantro.

Makes 4 servings

NOTE: This soup keeps well and is even more flavorful the next day.

Wild Rice and Asparagus Soup

½ cup instant wild rice

½ pound thin asparagus spears

1½ teaspoons margarine

1 shallot, minced *or* ¼ cup minced red onion

1 tablespoon all-purpose flour

1 cup low-sodium chicken broth

½ cup fat-free half-and-half

¼ teaspoon crushed dried thyme

⅛ teaspoon black pepper

1. Cook rice according to package directions. Drain. Set aside.

2. Meanwhile, trim asparagus. Place in skillet with water to cover. Cook over medium-high heat 5 minutes or until tender. Drain. Cut asparagus into 1-inch pieces. Set aside.

3. Melt margarine in medium saucepan over medium heat. Add shallot; cook 3 minutes or until tender, stirring occasionally. Stir in flour until absorbed. Stir in broth; cook 1 to 2 minutes or until slightly thickened. Add half-and-half, thyme and pepper. Stir in cooked rice and asparagus. Reduce heat to low; simmer 5 minutes.

Makes 4 servings

NOTE: If you prefer, you can cook regular wild rice instead of using instant. However, wild rice requires longer cooking than other rices. Avoid overcooking, because it will lose its characteristic chewy texture.

Curried Coconut Lentil Soup

1 tablespoon vegetable oil

1½ cups dried red lentils, rinsed and sorted

¼ cup minced onion

¼ cup unsweetened coconut, plus additional for garnish

3 tablespoons curry powder

2 tablespoons fresh parsley, chopped

1 teaspoon ground ginger

½ teaspoon garlic powder

½ teaspoon salt

½ teaspoon black pepper

1 container (48 ounces) vegetable broth

2 cups water

1. Heat oil in large saucepan over medium heat. Add lentils, onion, ¼ cup coconut, curry powder, parsley, ginger, garlic powder, salt and pepper; cook and stir 1 minute or until spices are fragrant.

2. Add broth and water; bring to a boil over high heat. Reduce heat to low. Simmer, uncovered, 20 minutes or until lentils are tender. Garnish with additional coconut.

Makes 4 servings

Greens, White Bean and Barley Soup

2 tablespoons olive oil

1½ cups chopped onions

3 carrots, diced

2 cloves garlic, minced

1½ cups sliced mushrooms

6 cups vegetable broth

2 cups cooked barley

1 can (about 15 ounces) Great Northern beans, rinsed and drained

2 bay leaves

1 teaspoon sugar

1 teaspoon dried thyme

7 cups chopped stemmed collard greens (about 24 ounces)

1 tablespoon white wine vinegar

Hot pepper sauce

Red bell pepper strips (optional)

1. Heat oil in Dutch oven over medium heat. Add onions, carrots and garlic; cook and stir 3 minutes. Add mushrooms; cook and stir 5 minutes or until carrots are tender.

2. Add broth, barley, beans, bay leaves, sugar and thyme; bring to a boil over high heat. Reduce heat to medium-low; cover and simmer 5 minutes. Add greens; simmer 10 minutes. Remove and discard bay leaves. Stir in vinegar. Season with hot pepper sauce. Garnish with red bell peppers.

Makes 8 servings

Two-Cheese Potato and Cauliflower Soup

1   tablespoon butter

1   cup chopped onion

2   cloves garlic, minced

5   cups whole milk

1   pound Yukon Gold potatoes,
    peeled and diced

1   pound cauliflower florets

1½ teaspoons salt

⅛   teaspoon ground red pepper

1½ cups (6 ounces) shredded sharp
    Cheddar cheese

⅓   cup crumbled blue cheese

1. Melt butter in large saucepan over medium-high heat. Add onion; cook and stir 4 minutes or until translucent. Add garlic; cook and stir 15 seconds. Add milk, potatoes, cauliflower, salt and red pepper; bring to a boil. Reduce heat to low. Cover tightly and simmer 15 minutes or until potatoes are tender. Cool slightly.

2. Working in batches, process soup in food processor or blender until smooth. Return to saucepan. Cook and stir over medium heat just until heated through. Remove from heat; stir in cheeses until melted.

Makes 4 to 6 servings

TIP: One pound of trimmed cauliflower will yield about 1½ cups of florets. You can also substitute 1 pound of frozen cauliflower florets for the fresh florets.

Chile Pepper & Corn Cream Chowder

2 tablespoons butter

1 cup chopped onion

2 Anaheim or poblano chile peppers,* seeded and diced

½ cup thinly sliced celery

1 package (16 ounces) frozen corn

12 ounces unpeeled new red potatoes, diced

4 cups whole milk

6 ounces cream cheese, cubed

2 teaspoons salt

¾ teaspoon black pepper

*Mild, with just the hint of a bite, Anaheim chiles are medium green peppers with a long narrow shape.

1. Melt butter in large saucepan over medium-high heat. Add onion, Anaheim peppers and celery; cook and stir 5 minutes or until onion is translucent.

2. Add corn, potatoes and milk. Bring to a boil. Reduce heat to medium-low; cover and simmer 10 minutes or until potatoes are tender.

3. Remove from heat; add cream cheese, salt and black pepper. Stir until cream cheese is melted.

Makes 4 to 6 servings

Ravioli Minestrone

1 package (7 ounces) refrigerated 3-cheese ravioli **or** 1 package (9 ounces) reduced-fat 4-cheese ravioli

2 teaspoons olive oil

2 carrots, chopped

1 medium onion, chopped

1 stalk celery, chopped

2 cloves garlic, minced

6 cups water

1 can (about 15 ounces) chickpeas, rinsed and drained

1 can (about 14 ounces) diced tomatoes

3 tablespoons tomato paste

1 teaspoon dried basil

1 teaspoon dried oregano

¾ teaspoon salt

¾ teaspoon black pepper

1 medium zucchini, cut in half lengthwise and sliced (about 2 cups)

1 package (10 ounces) baby spinach

1. Cook ravioli according to package directions. Drain; keep warm.

2. Meanwhile, heat oil in Dutch oven over medium-high heat. Add carrots, onion, celery and garlic; cook, stirring occasionally, about 5 minutes or until vegetables are softened.

3. Stir in water, chickpeas, tomatoes, tomato paste, basil, oregano, salt and pepper. Bring to a boil; reduce heat and simmer 15 minutes or until vegetables are tender. Add zucchini; cook 5 minutes. Stir in spinach; cook 2 minutes or just until spinach is wilted. Stir in ravioli.

Makes 8 servings

Italian Mushroom Soup

½ cup dried porcini mushrooms (about ½ ounce)

1 tablespoon olive oil

2 cups chopped onions

8 ounces sliced cremini or button mushrooms, plus additional for garnish

2 cloves garlic, minced

¼ teaspoon dried thyme

¼ cup all-purpose flour

4 cups vegetable broth

½ cup whipping cream

⅓ cup Marsala wine (optional)

Salt and black pepper

1. Place dried mushrooms in small bowl; cover with boiling water. Let stand 15 minutes or until tender.

2. Meanwhile, heat oil in large saucepan over medium heat. Add onions; cook 5 minutes or until translucent, stirring occasionally. Add 8 ounces cremini mushrooms, garlic and thyme; cook 8 minutes, stirring occasionally. Add flour; cook and stir 1 minute. Stir in broth.

3. Drain porcini mushrooms, reserving liquid. Chop mushrooms; add to saucepan with reserved liquid. Bring to a boil. Reduce heat to medium-low; simmer 10 minutes. Cool completely. Working in batches, process soup in food processor or blender until smooth. Return to saucepan over medium-low heat. Stir in cream and Marsala, if desired; season with salt and pepper. Simmer 5 minutes or until heated through. Garnish with reserved mushrooms.

Makes 6 to 8 servings

Carrot & Coriander Soup

¼ cup (½ stick) butter or margarine

4 cups grated carrots (about 1 pound)

1 cup finely chopped onion

3 cups chicken broth

2 tablespoons lemon juice

1½ teaspoons ground coriander

1½ teaspoons ground cumin

1 clove garlic, minced

2 tablespoons finely chopped fresh coriander (cilantro)

Salt and black pepper

1. Melt butter in medium saucepan over medium-high heat. Add carrots and onion; cook and stir 5 minutes or until softened. Add broth, lemon juice, ground coriander, cumin and garlic. Bring to a boil over high heat. Reduce heat to low; cover and simmer 25 to 30 minutes.

2. Process soup in batches in food processor or blender until smooth. Stir in fresh coriander. Season with salt and pepper. Serve immediately or cool and store up to 1 week in refrigerator. Reheat before serving.

Makes 4 to 6 servings

Sweet Pepper Garlic Soup

2 teaspoons olive oil

½ cup chopped onion

6 cloves garlic, chopped

1 cup cubed unpeeled potato

1 cup chopped red bell pepper

3½ cups fat-free reduced-sodium chicken broth

1 cup low-fat (1%) cottage cheese

2 tablespoons plain nonfat yogurt

⅛ teaspoon black pepper

Fresh parsley and bell pepper strips (optional)

1. Heat oil in medium saucepan over medium heat; add onion and garlic. Cook and stir 3 minutes or until onion is tender.

2. Add potato, bell pepper and broth. Bring to a boil; reduce heat and simmer 10 to 15 minutes or until potato is easily pierced when tested with fork. Remove from heat; cool completely.

3. Place broth mixture in food processor or blender; process until smooth. Refrigerate until completely cool.

4. Place cottage cheese and yogurt in food processor or blender; process until smooth. Set aside ¼ cup cheese mixture. Stir remaining cheese mixture into chilled broth mixture until well blended. Add black pepper; mix well. Top with reserved cheese mixture. Garnish with parsley and bell pepper strips, if desired.

Makes 6 servings

Potato and Leek Soup

4 cups chicken broth

3 potatoes, peeled and diced

1½ cups chopped cabbage

1 leek, diced

1 onion, chopped

2 carrots, diced

1 teaspoon salt

½ teaspoon caraway seeds

½ teaspoon black pepper

1 bay leaf

½ cup sour cream

1 pound bacon, crisp-cooked and crumbled

¼ cup chopped fresh parsley

Slow Cooker Directions

1. Combine broth, potatoes, cabbage, leek, onion, carrots, salt, caraway seeds, pepper and bay leaf in slow cooker; mix well.

2. Cover; cook on LOW 8 to 10 hours or on HIGH 4 to 5 hours.

3. Remove and discard bay leaf. Whisk ½ cup hot liquid from slow cooker into sour cream in small bowl until blended. Add sour cream mixture and bacon to slow cooker; mix well. Sprinkle with parsley.

Makes 6 to 8 servings

Hearty Mushroom Barley Soup

1   teaspoon extra virgin olive oil

2   cups chopped onions

1   cup thinly sliced carrots

2   cans (about 14 ounces each) fat-free reduced-sodium chicken broth

12 ounces sliced mushrooms

1   can (10¾ ounces) 98% fat-free cream of mushroom soup, undiluted

½   cup uncooked quick-cooking barley

1   teaspoon reduced-sodium Worcestershire sauce

½   teaspoon dried thyme

¼   cup finely chopped green onions

¼   teaspoon salt

¼   teaspoon black pepper

1. Coat Dutch oven or large saucepan with nonstick cooking spray; heat over medium-high heat until hot. Add oil and tilt pan to coat bottom of pan. Add onions; cook and stir 8 minutes or until onions just begin to turn golden. Add carrots and cook and stir 2 minutes.

2. Add broth, mushrooms, soup, barley, Worcestershire sauce and thyme; bring to a boil over high heat. Reduce heat; cover and simmer 15 minutes, stirring occasionally. Stir in green onions, salt and pepper.

Makes 4 servings

Exotic Mushroom Soup

6 tablespoons (¾ stick) butter, divided

1 small onion, finely chopped

4 cups water, divided

3 teaspoons instant chicken bouillon granules

8 ounces fresh assorted exotic mushrooms, such as cèpes, shiitake, oyster, portobello, cremini, morels or chanterelles *or* 8 ounces button mushrooms, sliced

1 teaspoon lemon juice

4 tablespoons all-purpose flour

¼ teaspoon white pepper

1 cup half-and-half or whipping cream

Fresh chives (optional)

1. Heat 2 tablespoons butter in large saucepan over medium-high heat until melted and bubbly. Add onion; cook and stir 3 minutes or until softened. Add 3½ cups water and bouillon; cover and bring to a boil over high heat. Reduce heat to medium-low.

2. Meanwhile, slice stems and caps of shiitake, chanterelle or morel mushrooms; add to broth mixture. Thinly slice stems of cèpes, oyster, portobello or cremini mushrooms; reserve caps.* Add to broth mixture; simmer 10 minutes.

3. Slice reserved mushroom caps. Heat 2 tablespoons butter in medium skillet over medium-high heat until melted and bubbly. Add mushroom caps; cook and stir just until softened. Remove to broth mixture with slotted spoon.

4. Add remaining 2 tablespoons butter and lemon juice to same skillet; stir until butter is melted. Stir in flour and pepper until smooth. Stir in remaining ½ cup water until blended. Add to broth mixture; cook until soup thickens, stirring constantly. Stir in half-and-half. Garnish with chives.

If using button mushrooms, slice lengthwise through caps and stems; add to broth mixture.

Makes 6 servings

Curried Parsnip Soup

1½ pounds parsnips, peeled and cut into 2-inch pieces

1 tablespoon olive oil

1 tablespoon butter

½ medium yellow onion, chopped

1 stalk celery, diced

2 cloves garlic, minced

1½ teaspoons salt

1 teaspoon curry powder

¼ teaspoon grated fresh ginger

¼ teaspoon freshly ground black pepper

4 cups reduced-sodium chicken or vegetable broth

Toasted bread slices (optional)

Chopped fresh chives (optional)

1. Preheat oven to 400°F. Line large baking sheet with foil.

2. Combine parsnips and oil in large bowl; toss to coat. Spread in single layer on prepared baking sheet. Bake 35 to 45 minutes or until parsnips are tender and lightly browned around edges, stirring once halfway through cooking.

3. Melt butter in large saucepan over medium heat. Add onion and celery; cook and stir about 8 minutes or until onion is translucent and vegetables are tender. Add garlic, salt, curry powder, ginger and pepper; cook and stir 1 minute. Add parsnips and broth; bring to a boil over medium-high heat. Reduce heat to medium-low; cover and simmer 10 minutes.

4. Working in batches, process soup in blender or food processor until smooth. Transfer soup to large bowl. Serve with toasted bread, if desired. Garnish with chives.

Makes 4 to 6 servings

Curried Vegetable-Rice Soup

1 package (16 ounces) frozen stir-fry vegetables

1 can (about 14 ounces) vegetable broth

¾ cup uncooked instant brown rice

2 teaspoons curry powder

½ teaspoon salt

½ teaspoon hot pepper sauce

1 can (14 ounces) unsweetened coconut milk

1 tablespoon lime juice

1. Combine vegetables and broth in large saucepan. Cover; bring to a boil over high heat. Stir in rice, curry powder, salt and hot pepper sauce. Reduce heat to medium-low; cover and simmer 8 minutes or until rice is tender, stirring once.

2. Stir in coconut milk; cook 3 minutes or until heated through. Remove from heat; stir in lime juice. Serve immediately.

Makes 4 servings

LIGHTEN UP: For a lighter soup with less fat and fewer calories, substitute light unsweetened coconut milk. Most large supermarkets carry this in their international foods section.

Creamy Onion Soup

6 tablespoons (¾ stick) butter, divided

1 large sweet onion, thinly sliced (about 3 cups)

1 can (about 14 ounces) chicken broth

2 cubes chicken bouillon

¼ teaspoon black pepper

¼ cup all-purpose flour

1½ cups milk

1½ cups (6 ounces) shredded Colby-Jack cheese

Chopped fresh parsley (optional)

1. Melt 2 tablespoons butter in large saucepan or Dutch oven over medium heat. Add onion; cook 10 minutes or until soft and translucent, stirring occasionally. Add broth, bouillon and pepper; cook until bouillon is dissolved and mixture is heated through.

2. Meanwhile, melt remaining 4 tablespoons butter in medium saucepan. Whisk in flour; cook and stir 1 minute. Gradually whisk in milk until well blended. Cook 10 minutes or until very thick, stirring occasionally.

3. Add milk mixture to soup; cook over medium-low heat 5 to 10 minutes or until thickened, stirring occasionally. Add cheese; cook 5 minutes or until melted and smooth. Ladle into bowls; garnish with parsley.

Makes 4 servings

Baked Potato Soup

3 medium russet potatoes (about 1 pound)

¼ cup (½ stick) butter

1 cup chopped onion

½ cup all-purpose flour

4 cups chicken or vegetable broth

1½ cups instant mashed potato flakes

1 cup water

1 cup half-and-half

1 teaspoon salt

½ teaspoon dried basil

½ teaspoon dried thyme

¼ teaspoon black pepper

1 cup (4 ounces) shredded Cheddar cheese

4 slices bacon, crisp-cooked and crumbled

1 green onion, chopped

1. Preheat oven to 400°F. Scrub potatoes and prick in several places with fork. Place in baking pan; bake 1 hour. Cool completely; peel and cut into ½-inch pieces. (Potatoes can be prepared several days in advance; refrigerate until ready to use.)

2. Melt butter in large saucepan or Dutch oven over medium heat. Add onion; cook and stir 3 minutes or until softened. Whisk in flour; cook and stir 1 minute. Gradually whisk in broth until well blended. Stir in mashed potato flakes, water, half-and-half, salt, basil, thyme and pepper; bring to a boil over medium-high heat. Reduce heat to medium; cook 5 minutes.

3. Stir in baked potato cubes; cook 10 to 15 minutes or until soup is thickened and heated through. Ladle into bowls; top with cheese, bacon and green onion.

Makes 6 to 8 servings

Harvest Pumpkin Soup

1 sugar pumpkin or acorn squash
   (about 2 pounds)

1 kabocha or butternut squash
   (about 2 pounds)

   Salt and black pepper

2 tablespoons olive oil

2 tablespoons butter

1 large onion, finely chopped
   (about 1¾ cups)

1 medium carrot, chopped (½ cup)

2 stalks celery, chopped (½ cup)

¼ cup packed brown sugar

2 tablespoons tomato paste

1 tablespoon minced fresh ginger

1 clove garlic, minced

1 teaspoon salt

1 teaspoon ground cinnamon

¼ teaspoon ground cumin

¼ teaspoon black pepper

4 cups vegetable broth

1 cup milk

2 teaspoons lemon juice

   Roasted pumpkin seeds
   (optional, see Tip)

1. Preheat oven to 400°F. Line large baking sheet with foil; spray with nonstick cooking spray.

2. Cut pumpkin and kabocha squash in half; scoop out seeds and strings. Season cut sides with salt and pepper. Place cut sides down on large baking sheet; bake 30 to 45 minutes or until fork-tender. When squash is cool enough to handle, remove skin; chop flesh into 1-inch pieces.

3. Heat oil and butter in large saucepan over medium-high heat. Add onion, carrot and celery; cook and stir 5 minutes or until vegetables are tender. Add brown sugar, tomato paste, ginger, garlic, 1 teaspoon salt, cinnamon, cumin and ¼ teaspoon pepper; cook and stir 1 minute. Add broth and squash; bring to a boil. Reduce heat to medium; cook 20 minutes or until squash is very soft.

4. Blend soup with immersion blender until desired consistency. (Or, process in batches in food processor or blender.) Stir in milk and lemon juice; heat through. Garnish with pumpkin seeds.

Makes 8 servings

TIP: Roasted pumpkin seeds can be found at many supermarkets, or you can roast the seeds that you remove from the pumpkin (and the squash) in the recipe. Combine the seeds with 2 teaspoons vegetable oil and ⅛ teaspoon salt in a small bowl; toss to coat. Spread in a single layer on a small foil-lined baking sheet; bake at 300°F 20 to 25 minutes or until the seeds begin to brown, stirring once.

Creamy Tomato Soup

3 tablespoons olive oil, divided

2 tablespoons butter

1 large onion, finely chopped

2 cloves garlic, minced

2 teaspoons sugar

1 teaspoon salt

½ teaspoon dried oregano

2 cans (28 ounces each) peeled Italian plum tomatoes

4 cups ½-inch focaccia cubes (half of 9-ounce loaf)

½ teaspoon freshly ground black pepper

½ cup whipping cream

1. Heat 2 tablespoons oil and butter in large saucepan over medium-high heat. Add onion; cook and stir 5 minutes or until softened. Add garlic, sugar, salt and oregano; cook 30 seconds. Add tomatoes with juice; bring to a boil. Reduce heat to medium-low; simmer 45 minutes, stirring occasionally.

2. Meanwhile, prepare croutons. Preheat oven to 350°F. Combine focaccia cubes, remaining 1 tablespoon oil and pepper in large bowl; toss to coat. Spread on large rimmed baking sheet. Bake about 10 minutes or until bread cubes are golden brown.

3. Blend soup with immersion blender or in batches in food processor or blender. Stir in cream; heat through. Serve soup topped with croutons.

Makes 6 servings

Garden Vegetable Soup

1 tablespoon olive oil

1 medium onion, chopped

1 carrot, chopped

1 stalk celery, chopped

1 medium zucchini, diced

1 medium yellow squash, diced

1 red bell pepper, diced

2 tablespoons tomato paste

2 cloves garlic, minced

2 teaspoons salt

1 teaspoon Italian seasoning

½ teaspoon black pepper

8 cups vegetable broth

1 can (28 ounces) whole tomatoes, chopped, juice reserved

½ cup uncooked pearl barley

1 cup cut green beans (1-inch pieces)

½ cup corn

¼ cup slivered fresh basil

1 tablespoon lemon juice

1. Heat oil in large saucepan or Dutch oven over medium-high heat. Add onion, carrot and celery; cook and stir 8 minutes or until softened. Add zucchini, yellow squash and bell pepper; cook and stir 5 minutes or until softened. Stir in tomato paste, garlic, salt, Italian seasoning and black pepper; cook 1 minute. Add broth and tomatoes with juice; bring to a boil. Stir in barley.

2. Reduce heat to low; cook 30 minutes. Stir in green beans and corn; cook about 15 minutes or until barley is tender and green beans are crisp-tender. Stir in basil and lemon juice.

Makes 8 to 10 servings

Kale and White Bean Soup

2 slices reduced-sodium bacon, chopped

½ cup diced onion

1 unpeeled new red potato, diced

2 cans (about 14 ounces each) reduced-sodium vegetable broth

1 teaspoon minced garlic

½ teaspoon dried oregano

2 bay leaves

1 can (14½ ounces) low-sodium sliced carrots, drained

1 can (13½ ounces) kale or spinach, drained

1 can (10 ounces) reduced-sodium white kidney beans, rinsed and drained

⅓ cup finely chopped sun-dried tomato strips, packed in olive oil

1 tablespoon olive oil

¼ teaspoon black pepper

⅛ teaspoon salt

1. Cook bacon in large saucepan over medium heat until crisp. Drain off excess fat.

2. Add onion and potato to saucepan; cook and stir 10 minutes or until onion is browned. Stir in broth, garlic, oregano and bay leaves; bring to a simmer. Cover and simmer 5 minutes or until potato is tender.

3. Add carrots, kale, beans and sun-dried tomatoes; cook 5 minutes. Remove and discard bay leaves. Stir in oil, pepper and salt.

Makes 6 servings

QUICK & EASY

Quick Tuscan Bean, Tomato and Spinach Soup

2 cans (about 14 ounces each) diced tomatoes with onions

1 can (about 14 ounces) fat-free reduced-sodium chicken broth

2 teaspoons sugar

2 teaspoons dried basil

¾ teaspoon reduced-sodium Worcestershire sauce

1 can (about 15 ounces) small white beans, rinsed and drained

3 ounces fresh baby spinach leaves or chopped spinach leaves, stems removed

2 teaspoons extra virgin olive oil

1. Combine tomatoes, broth, sugar, basil and Worcestershire sauce in Dutch oven or large saucepan; bring to a boil over high heat. Reduce heat to low. Simmer, uncovered, 10 minutes.

2. Stir in beans and spinach; cook 5 minutes or until spinach is tender.

3. Remove from heat; stir in oil just before serving.

Makes 4 servings

Quick Hot and Sour Chicken Soup

2 cups water

2 cups chicken broth

1 package (about 10 ounces) refrigerated fully cooked chicken breast strips, cut into bite-size pieces

1 package (about 7 ounces) chicken-flavored rice and vermicelli mix

1 jalapeño pepper,* minced

2 green onions, chopped

1 tablespoon soy sauce

1 tablespoon lime juice

1 tablespoon minced fresh cilantro

Jalapeño peppers can sting and irritate the skin, so wear rubber gloves when handling peppers and do not touch your eyes.

1. Combine water, broth, chicken, rice mix, jalapeño pepper, green onions and soy sauce in large saucepan; bring to a boil over high heat. Reduce heat to low. Cover; simmer 20 minutes or until rice is tender, stirring occasionally.

2. Stir in lime juice and sprinkle with cilantro.

Makes 4 servings

Chicken Tortellini Soup

6 cups chicken broth

1 package (9 ounces) refrigerated cheese and spinach tortellini

1 package (about 6 ounces) refrigerated fully cooked chicken breast strips, cut into bite-size pieces

2 cups baby spinach

4 to 6 tablespoons grated Parmesan cheese

1 tablespoon chopped fresh chives *or* 2 tablespoons sliced green onion

1. Bring broth to a boil in large saucepan over high heat; add tortellini. Reduce heat to medium; cook 5 minutes. Stir in chicken and spinach.

2. Reduce heat to low; cook 3 minutes or until chicken is heated through. Sprinkle with Parmesan and chives.

Makes 4 servings

Sweet Potato Bisque with Ginger

2 cans (15 ounces each) sweet potatoes in heavy syrup, drained

1 can (about 13 ounces) coconut milk

1 cup vegetable or chicken broth

1 green onion, cut into thirds

¼ teaspoon salt

⅛ teaspoon ground red pepper

2 teaspoons grated fresh ginger *or* crystallized ginger, plus additional for garnish

Fresh chives (optional)

1. Combine sweet potatoes, coconut milk, broth, green onion, salt and red pepper in food processor or blender; process until smooth.

2. Transfer to large saucepan. Bring to a boil, stirring frequently. Reduce heat to medium-low; simmer 3 minutes. Remove from heat; stir in 2 teaspoons ginger. Garnish with additional ginger and chives.

Makes 4 servings

Long Soup

1½ tablespoons vegetable oil

¼ small head cabbage, shredded

8 ounces boneless lean pork, cut into thin strips

6 cups chicken broth

2 tablespoons soy sauce

½ teaspoon minced fresh ginger

8 green onions, cut diagonally into ½-inch slices

4 ounces uncooked Chinese-style thin egg noodles

1. Heat oil in wok or large skillet over medium-high heat. Add cabbage and pork; stir-fry about 5 minutes or until pork is no longer pink in center.

2. Add broth, soy sauce and ginger. Bring to a boil. Reduce heat to low; simmer 10 minutes, stirring occasionally. Stir in green onions.

3. Add noodles; cook 2 to 4 minutes or until noodles are tender.

Makes 4 servings

Quick & Easy Meatball Soup

1   package (15 to 18 ounces) frozen
    Italian sausage meatballs
    without sauce

2   cans (about 14 ounces each)
    Italian-style stewed tomatoes

2   cans (about 14 ounces each) beef
    broth

1   can (about 14 ounces) mixed
    vegetables

½   cup uncooked rotini pasta or
    small macaroni

½   teaspoon dried oregano

1. Thaw meatballs in microwave according to package directions.

2. Place tomatoes, broth, mixed vegetables, pasta and oregano in large saucepan. Add meatballs; bring to a boil over medium-high heat. Reduce heat to medium-low. Simmer, covered, 15 minutes or until pasta is tender.

Makes 4 to 6 servings

Quick Broccoli Soup

4 cups fat-free reduced-sodium chicken or vegetable broth

2½ pounds broccoli florets

1 onion, quartered

1 cup low-fat (1%) milk

¼ teaspoon salt (optional)

¼ cup crumbled blue cheese

1. Place broth, broccoli and onion in large saucepan; bring to a boil over high heat. Reduce heat to low; cover and simmer about 20 minutes or until vegetables are tender.

2. Process soup in blender and return to saucepan. Add milk and salt, if desired. Add water or additional broth, if needed.

3. Ladle soup into serving bowls; sprinkle with cheese.

Makes 6 servings

Easy-As-Pie Holiday Soup

1 teaspoon canola oil

½ cup diced onion (½ medium onion)

1 cup peeled diced apple (1 medium apple)

¾ teaspoon pumpkin pie spice

¼ teaspoon salt

¼ teaspoon black pepper

½ cup fat-free reduced-sodium chicken broth

1 box (12 ounces) frozen cooked winter squash, thawed (see Tips)

1 cup fat-free evaporated milk

4 tablespoons fat-free sour cream (optional)

Pumpkin pie spice (optional)

1. Heat oil in large saucepan over medium-low heat. Add onion. Cook and stir 3 minutes or until onion is translucent. **Do not brown**. Add apple, pumpkin pie spice, salt and pepper. Cook and stir 1 minute to coat apple. Add broth. Simmer, uncovered, 8 to 10 minutes or until apple is tender and most of the broth has evaporated.

2. Add thawed squash and milk to apple mixture. Simmer, uncovered, 6 to 8 minutes or until flavors are blended and soup is hot. Ladle into bowls. Garnish with sour cream and additional pumpkin pie spice.

Makes 6 servings

TIP: To easily thaw frozen box of squash, place in microwavable container. Cover. Microwave on HIGH 3 minutes. Stir. Microwave 1 minute more if needed to thaw completely.

COOK'S NOTE: For added flavor, cook 1 clove garlic, minced, and 1 tablespoon minced, peeled, fresh ginger with the onion. Or add ¼ to ½ teaspoon mild curry powder with the pumpkin pie spice.

Pepperoni Pizza Soup

1 tablespoon oil

1 cup sliced mushrooms

1 cup chopped green bell pepper

½ cup chopped onion

1 can (15 ounces) pizza sauce

1 can (about 14 ounces) chicken
   broth

1 cup water

3 ounces sliced pepperoni

1 teaspoon dried oregano

1 cup (4 ounces) shredded
   mozzarella cheese

   Croutons (optional)

1. Heat oil in large saucepan over medium heat. Add mushrooms, bell pepper and onion. Cook, stirring frequently, 7 minutes or until vegetables are tender.

2. Stir in pizza sauce, broth, water, pepperoni and oregano. Bring to a boil. Reduce heat and simmer 5 minutes. Serve with cheese. Sprinkle with croutons, if desired.

Makes 4 servings

Tomato-Herb Soup

1   can (about 14 ounces) no-salt-added diced tomatoes

1   can (about 14 ounces) reduced-sodium chicken broth

1   package (8 ounces) frozen bell pepper stir-fry mixture

1   cup frozen green beans

½   cup water

1   tablespoon ketchup

1   to 2 teaspoons dried oregano

1   teaspoon dried basil

⅛   teaspoon red pepper flakes (optional)

Combine tomatoes, broth, bell peppers, green beans, water, ketchup, oregano, basil and red pepper flakes, if desired, in large saucepan. Bring to a boil over medium-high heat. Reduce heat to medium-low. Simmer, covered, 20 minutes or until beans are tender.

Makes 4 servings

VARIATION: Substitute chopped fresh bell peppers for the frozen stir-fry mix.

Asian Ramen Noodle Soup

2 cans (about 14 ounces each) fat-free reduced-sodium chicken broth

4 ounces boneless pork loin, cut into thin strips

¾ cup thinly sliced mushrooms

½ cup firm tofu, cut into ¼-inch cubes (optional)

3 tablespoons white vinegar

3 tablespoons dry sherry

1 tablespoon reduced-sodium soy sauce

½ teaspoon ground red pepper

1 package (3 ounces) ramen noodles, any flavor, broken*

1 egg, beaten

¼ cup finely chopped green onions, green tops only

Discard seasoning packet.

1. Bring broth to a boil in large saucepan over high heat; add pork, mushrooms and tofu, if desired. Reduce heat to medium-low; simmer, covered, 5 minutes. Stir in vinegar, sherry, soy sauce and red pepper.

2. Return broth mixture to a boil over high heat; stir in noodles. Cook, stirring occasionally, 5 to 7 minutes or until noodles are tender. Slowly stir in egg and green onions; remove from heat. Ladle soup into individual bowls.

Makes 4 servings

Wild Rice Soup

½ cup dried lentils, rinsed and sorted

1 package (6 ounces) long grain and wild rice blend

1 can (about 14 ounces) vegetable broth

1 bag (10 ounces) frozen mixed vegetables

1 cup milk

2 slices (1 ounce each) American cheese, cut into pieces

1. Place lentils in small saucepan; cover with about 3 cups water. Bring to a boil over medium-high heat. Reduce heat to low. Simmer, covered, 5 minutes. Let stand, covered, 1 hour. Drain and rinse lentils.

2. Cook rice according to package directions. Add lentils, broth, mixed vegetables, milk and cheese. Bring to a boil over medium-high heat. Reduce heat to low. Simmer, uncovered, 20 minutes.

Makes 6 servings

Tofu and Snow Pea Noodle Bowl

5 cups water

6 tablespoons chicken-flavored broth powder*

4 ounces uncooked vermicelli, broken in thirds

½ pound firm tofu, rinsed, patted dry and cut in ¼-inch cubes

1 cup (3 ounces) fresh snow peas

1 cup matchstick-size carrot strips**

½ teaspoon chili garlic sauce

½ cup chopped green onions

¼ cup chopped fresh cilantro (optional)

2 tablespoons lime juice

1 tablespoon grated fresh ginger

2 teaspoons soy sauce

Chicken-flavored vegetarian broth powder can be found in natural food stores and some supermarkets.

**Matchstick-size carrot strips are sometimes called shredded carrots and may be sold with other prepared vegetables in the supermarket produce section.*

1. Bring water to a boil in large saucepan over high heat. Stir in broth powder and vermicelli; return to a boil. Reduce heat to medium-high; simmer 6 minutes. Stir in tofu, snow peas, carrots and chili garlic sauce; simmer 2 minutes.

2. Remove from heat; stir in green onions, cilantro, if desired, lime juice, ginger and soy sauce. Serve immediately.

Makes 4 servings

Minestrone Soup

¾ cup uncooked small shell pasta

2 cans (about 14 ounces each) vegetable broth

1 can (28 ounces) crushed tomatoes in tomato purée

1 can (about 15 ounces) white beans, rinsed and drained

1 package (16 ounces) frozen vegetable medley, such as broccoli, green beans, carrots and red peppers

4 to 6 teaspoons prepared pesto

1. Cook pasta according to package directions; drain.

2. Meanwhile, combine broth, tomatoes and beans in large saucepan; bring to a boil over high heat. Reduce heat to low; cover and simmer 3 to 5 minutes.

3. Add vegetables to broth mixture; return to a boil over high heat. Stir in pasta; simmer, uncovered, until vegetables are tender. Ladle soup into bowls; Top each serving with about 1 teaspoon pesto.

Makes 4 to 6 servings

Pesto & Tortellini Soup

1   package (9 ounces) refrigerated cheese tortellini

3   cans (about 14 ounces each) chicken or vegetable broth

1   jar (7 ounces) roasted red peppers, drained and thinly sliced

¾   cup frozen green peas

3   to 4 cups packed stemmed fresh spinach

1   to 2 tablespoons prepared pesto

Grated Parmesan cheese (optional)

1. Cook tortellini according to package directions; drain.

2. Meanwhile, bring broth to a boil in large saucepan or Dutch oven over high heat. Add cooked tortellini, roasted peppers and peas; return to a boil. Reduce heat to medium; simmer 1 minute.

3. Remove from heat; stir in spinach and pesto. Garnish with Parmesan.

Makes 6 servings

NOTE: To easily remove stems from spinach leaves, fold each leaf in half, then pull stem toward top of leaf. Discard stems.

Egg Drop Soup

2 cans (about 14 ounces each) fat-free reduced-sodium chicken broth

1 tablespoon reduced-sodium soy sauce

2 teaspoons cornstarch

½ cup cholesterol-free egg substitute

¼ cup thinly sliced green onions

1. Bring broth to a boil in large saucepan over high heat. Reduce heat to medium-low.

2. Whisk soy sauce and cornstarch in small bowl until smooth and well blended; stir into broth. Cook and stir 2 minutes or until slightly thickened.

3. Stirring constantly in one direction, slowly pour egg substitute in thin stream into soup.

4. Ladle soup into bowls; sprinkle with green onions.

Makes 2 servings

GLOBAL FLAVORS

Russian Borscht

4 cups thinly sliced green cabbage

1½ pounds beets, shredded

5 carrots, halved lengthwise and cut into 1-inch pieces

1 parsnip, halved lengthwise and cut into 1-inch pieces

1 cup chopped onion

4 cloves garlic, minced

1 pound beef stew meat, cut into ½-inch cubes

1 can (about 14 ounces) diced tomatoes

3 cans (about 14 ounces each) reduced-sodium beef broth

¼ cup lemon juice

1 tablespoon sugar

1 teaspoon black pepper

Sour cream (optional)

Chopped fresh parsley (optional)

Slow Cooker Directions

1. Layer cabbage, beets, carrots, parsnip, onion, garlic, beef, tomatoes, broth, lemon juice, sugar and pepper in slow cooker. Cover; cook on LOW 7 to 9 hours.

2. Season with additional lemon juice and sugar, if desired. Top with sour cream and sprinkle with parsley just before serving, if desired.

Makes 12 servings

Chicken Soup au Pistou

½ pound boneless skinless chicken breasts, cut into ½-inch pieces

1 large onion, diced

3 cans (about 14 ounces each) chicken broth

1 can (about 15 ounces) Great Northern beans, rinsed and drained

1 can (about 14 ounces) whole tomatoes, undrained

2 carrots, sliced

1 large potato, diced

¼ teaspoon salt

¼ teaspoon black pepper

1 cup fresh or frozen green beans, cut into 1-inch pieces

¼ cup prepared pesto

Grated Parmesan cheese (optional)

1. Spray large saucepan with olive oil cooking spray; heat over medium-high heat. Add chicken; cook and stir 5 minutes or until browned. Add onion; cook and stir 2 minutes.

2. Add broth, Great Northern beans, tomatoes, carrots, potato, salt and pepper. Bring to a boil, stirring to break up tomatoes. Reduce heat to low. Cover and simmer 15 minutes, stirring occasionally. Add green beans; cook 5 minutes or until vegetables are tender.

3. Ladle soup into bowls. Top each serving with 1½ teaspoons pesto and sprinkle with Parmesan cheese, if desired.

Makes 8 servings

Mediterranean Fish Soup

4 ounces uncooked pastina or other small pasta

¾ cup chopped onion

2 cloves garlic, minced

1 teaspoon whole fennel seeds

1 can (about 14 ounces) no-salt-added stewed tomatoes

1 can (about 14 ounces) fat-free reduced-sodium chicken broth

1 tablespoon minced fresh Italian parsley

½ teaspoon black pepper

¼ teaspoon ground turmeric

8 ounces firm, white-fleshed fish, cut into 1-inch pieces

3 ounces small raw shrimp, peeled (with tails on)

1. Cook pasta according to package directions, omitting salt. Drain.

2. Spray large saucepan with nonstick cooking spray; heat over medium heat. Add onion, garlic and fennel seeds; cook and stir 3 minutes or until onion is crisp-tender.

3. Stir in tomatoes, broth, parsley, pepper and turmeric; bring to a boil. Reduce heat to low; simmer 10 minutes.

4. Stir fish into saucepan; cook 1 minute. Add shrimp; cook until shrimp are pink and opaque. Divide pasta evenly among four bowls; ladle soup evenly over pasta.

Makes 4 servings

Turkey Albondigas Soup

¼ cup uncooked brown rice

Meatballs

½ pound ground lean turkey

1 tablespoon minced onion

1 teaspoon chopped fresh cilantro

1 teaspoon fat-free (skim) milk

½ teaspoon hot pepper sauce

⅛ teaspoon dried oregano

⅛ teaspoon black pepper

Broth

1 teaspoon olive oil

2 tablespoons chopped onion

1 clove garlic, minced

2½ cups fat-free low-sodium chicken broth

2 teaspoons hot pepper sauce

1 teaspoon tomato paste

⅛ teaspoon black pepper

3 small carrots, cut into rounds (about 1 cup)

½ medium zucchini, quartered lengthwise and cut crosswise into ½-inch slices

½ yellow crookneck squash, quartered lengthwise and cut crosswise into ½-inch slices

Garnish

Lime wedges

Fresh cilantro leaves

1. Prepare rice according to package directions, omitting salt and fat.

2. Meanwhile, combine turkey, 1 tablespoon minced onion, 1 teaspoon chopped cilantro, milk, ½ teaspoon hot pepper sauce, oregano and ⅛ teaspoon black pepper in medium bowl. Mix lightly until blended. Shape mixture into 1-inch balls.

3. For broth, heat oil in large saucepan over medium heat. Add 2 tablespoons onion and garlic; cook and stir until golden. Add broth, 2 teaspoons hot pepper sauce, tomato paste and ⅛ teaspoon black pepper. Bring to a boil over high heat; reduce to simmer.

4. Add meatballs and carrots to broth; simmer 15 minutes. Add zucchini, squash and cooked rice. Simmer 5 to 10 minutes or just until vegetables are tender.

5. Serve immediately. Garnish with lime wedges and cilantro leaves.

Makes 2 servings

Greek Lemon and Rice Soup

3 cans (about 14 ounces each) chicken broth

½ cup uncooked long-grain rice

3 egg yolks

¼ cup fresh lemon juice

Salt and black pepper

4 thin slices lemon (optional)

4 teaspoons finely chopped fresh Italian parsley (optional)

Slow Cooker Directions

1. Stir together chicken broth and rice in 4-quart slow cooker. Cover; cook on HIGH 2 to 3 hours or until rice is tender and fully cooked.

2. **Turn slow cooker to LOW.** Whisk together egg yolks and lemon juice in medium bowl. Add large spoonful of hot rice mixture to egg yolk mixture and whisk together briefly, then whisk this mixture back into remaining rice mixture. Cover; cook on LOW 10 minutes.

3. Season with salt and pepper. Garnish with lemon slices and parsley.

Makes 4 servings

Middle Eastern Chicken Soup

1   can (about 14 ounces) low-fat reduced-sodium chicken broth

1   can (about 15 ounces) chickpeas, rinsed and drained

1   cup chopped cooked chicken

1   small onion, chopped

1   carrot, chopped

1   clove garlic, minced

1   teaspoon dried oregano

1   teaspoon ground cumin

½   of 10-ounce package fresh spinach, stemmed and coarsely chopped

⅛   teaspoon black pepper

1. Combine broth, 1½ cans water, chickpeas, chicken, onion, carrot, garlic, oregano and cumin in medium saucepan. Bring to a boil over high heat. Reduce heat to medium-low; cover and simmer 15 minutes.

2. Stir in spinach and pepper; simmer, uncovered, 2 minutes or until wilted.

Makes 4 servings

Albondigas Soup

1 pound ground beef

½ small onion, finely chopped

1 egg

¼ cup dry bread crumbs

1 tablespoon chili powder

1 teaspoon ground cumin

½ teaspoon salt

3 cans (about 14 ounces each) chicken broth

1 medium carrot, thinly sliced

1 package (10 ounces) frozen corn *or* thawed frozen leaf spinach

¼ cup dry sherry

1. Mix ground beef, onion, egg, bread crumbs, chili powder, cumin and salt in medium bowl until well blended. Place mixture on lightly oiled cutting board; pat evenly into 1-inch-thick square. Cut into 36 squares with sharp knife; shape each square into a ball.

2. Place meatballs slightly apart in single layer in microwavable container. Cover loosely with waxed paper. Cook on HIGH 3 minutes or until meatballs are just barely pink in center.

3. Meanwhile, combine broth and carrot in large saucepan. Cover; bring to a boil over high heat. Stir in corn and sherry. Transfer meatballs to broth with slotted spoon. Reduce heat to medium; simmer 3 to 4 minutes or until meatballs are cooked through.

Makes 6 servings

NOTE: For extra flavor, sprinkle chopped fresh cilantro over hot soup.

Caribbean Callaloo Soup

1 teaspoon olive oil

1 large onion, chopped

4 cloves garlic, minced

¾ pound boneless skinless chicken breasts, thinly sliced crosswise

1½ pounds butternut squash, cut into ½-inch cubes

3 cans (about 14 ounces each) fat-free reduced-sodium chicken broth

2 jalapeño peppers,* seeded and minced

2 teaspoons dried thyme

½ of 10-ounce package fresh spinach, stemmed and torn

¼ cup plus 2 tablespoons shredded sweetened coconut**

Jalapeño peppers can sting and irritate the skin, so wear rubber gloves when handling peppers and do not touch your eyes.

**To toast coconut, spread in a single layer in heavy-bottomed skillet. Cook and stir 1 to 2 minutes or until lightly browned. Remove from skillet immediately.*

1. Heat oil in large nonstick skillet over medium-low heat. Add onion and garlic; cook and stir 5 minutes or until onion is tender. Add chicken; cover and cook 5 to 7 minutes or until chicken is no longer pink in center.

2. Add squash, broth, jalapeño peppers and thyme; bring to a boil over medium-high heat. Reduce heat to low. Simmer, covered, 15 to 20 minutes or until squash is very tender.

3. Remove skillet from heat; stir in spinach until wilted. Ladle into bowls and sprinkle with toasted coconut.

Makes 6 servings

Indian Carrot Soup

⅔ cup chopped onion (about 1 small)

1 tablespoon minced fresh ginger

1 teaspoon olive oil

1½ teaspoons curry powder

½ teaspoon ground cumin

2 cans (about 14 ounces each) fat-free reduced-sodium chicken broth, divided

1 pound peeled baby carrots

1 tablespoon sugar

¼ teaspoon ground cinnamon

Pinch ground red pepper

2 teaspoons fresh lime juice

3 tablespoons chopped fresh cilantro

¼ cup plain nonfat yogurt

1. Spray large saucepan with nonstick cooking spray; heat over medium heat. Add onion and ginger; reduce heat to low. Cover; cook 3 to 4 minutes or until onion is transparent and crisp-tender, stirring occasionally. Add oil; cook and stir, uncovered, 3 to 4 minutes or until onion just turns golden. Add curry powder and cumin; cook and stir 30 seconds or until fragrant. Add 1 can chicken broth and carrots; bring to a boil over high heat. Reduce heat to low; simmer, covered, 15 minutes or until carrots are tender.

2. Ladle carrot mixture into food processor; process until smooth. Return to saucepan; stir in remaining 1 can chicken broth, sugar, cinnamon and red pepper; bring to a boil over medium heat. Remove from heat; stir in lime juice. Ladle into bowls; sprinkle with cilantro. Top each serving with 1 tablespoon yogurt.

Makes 4 servings

Vietnamese Beef Soup (Pho)

¾ pound boneless beef top sirloin or top round steak

4 ounces thin rice noodles (rice sticks)

6 cups beef broth

3 cups water

2 tablespoons minced fresh ginger

2 tablespoons reduced-sodium soy sauce

1 cinnamon stick (3 inches long)

½ cup thinly sliced carrots

2 cups fresh bean sprouts

1 red onion, halved and thinly sliced

½ cup chopped fresh cilantro

½ cup chopped fresh basil

2 minced jalapeño peppers* *or* 1 to 3 teaspoons chili sauce

*Jalapeño peppers can sting and irritate the skin, so wear rubber gloves when handling peppers and do not touch your eyes.

1. Freeze beef 45 minutes or until firm. Place rice noodles in large bowl. Cover with hot water; soak 20 minutes or until soft. Drain.

2. Meanwhile, combine broth, water, ginger, soy sauce and cinnamon stick in large saucepan. Bring to a boil over high heat. Reduce heat to low; cover and simmer 20 minutes. Remove and discard cinnamon stick.

3. Slice beef lengthwise in half, then crosswise into very thin strips. Add noodles and carrots to simmering broth; cook 2 to 3 minutes or until carrots are tender. Add beef and bean sprouts; cook 1 minute or until beef is no longer pink.

4. Remove from heat; stir in red onion, cilantro, basil and jalapeño peppers.

Makes 6 servings

TIP: Rice noodles are semi-translucent dried noodles that come in many sizes and have many names, including rice stick noodles, rice-flour noodles and pho noodles. Widths range from very thin (called rice vermicelli) to 1 inch wide. All rice noodles must be soaked to soften and all may be used interchangeably.

Moroccan Lentil & Vegetable Soup

1 tablespoon olive oil

1 cup chopped onion

4 cloves garlic, minced

½ cup dried lentils, rinsed and sorted

1½ teaspoons ground coriander

1½ teaspoons ground cumin

½ teaspoon ground cinnamon

½ teaspoon black pepper

1 container (32 ounces) low-sodium vegetable broth

½ cup chopped celery

½ cup chopped sun-dried tomatoes (not packed in oil)

1 yellow squash, chopped

½ cup chopped green bell pepper

1 cup chopped plum tomatoes

½ cup chopped fresh Italian parsley

¼ cup chopped fresh cilantro *or* basil

1. Heat oil in medium saucepan over medium-high heat. Add onion and garlic; cook and stir 4 minutes or until onion is tender. Stir in lentils, coriander, cumin, cinnamon and black pepper; cook 2 minutes. Add broth, celery and sun-dried tomatoes; bring to a boil. Reduce heat to medium-low; cover and simmer 25 minutes.

2. Stir in squash and bell pepper; cover and cook 10 minutes or until lentils are tender.

3. Top with plum tomatoes, parsley and cilantro just before serving.

Makes 6 servings

TIP: Many soups, including this one, taste even better the next day after the flavors have had time to blend. Cover and refrigerate the soup overnight, reserving the plum tomatoes, parsley and cilantro until ready to serve.

Mexican Tortilla Soup

6 to 8 (6-inch) corn tortillas, preferably day-old

2 large very ripe tomatoes (about 1 pound), peeled, seeded and cut into chunks

⅔ cup coarsely chopped white onion

1 clove garlic

Vegetable oil

7 cups chicken broth

4 sprigs fresh cilantro

3 sprigs fresh mint (optional)

½ to 1 teaspoon salt

4 or 5 dried pasilla chiles

5 ounces queso Chihuahua *or* Monterey Jack cheese, cut into ½-inch cubes

¼ cup coarsely chopped fresh cilantro

1. Stack tortillas; cut stack into ½-inch-wide strips. Let tortilla strips stand, uncovered, on wire rack 1 to 2 hours to dry slightly.

2. Combine tomatoes, onion and garlic in blender or food processor; blend until smooth. Heat 3 tablespoons oil in large saucepan over medium heat until hot. Add tomato mixture; cook 10 minutes, stirring frequently. Add broth and cilantro sprigs; bring to a boil over high heat. Reduce heat to low; simmer, uncovered, 20 minutes. Add mint, if desired, and salt; simmer 10 minutes. Remove and discard cilantro and mint sprigs. Keep soup warm.

3. Heat ½ inch oil in large deep skillet over medium-high heat to 375°F; adjust heat to maintain temperature. Fry half of tortilla strips at a time, in single layer, 1 minute or until crisp, turning occasionally. Remove with slotted spoon; drain on paper towel-lined plate.

4. Fry chiles in same oil about 30 seconds or until puffed and crisp, turning occasionally. *Do not burn chiles.* Drain on paper towel-lined plate. Cool slightly; crumble into coarse pieces.

5. Ladle soup into bowls; serve with chiles, tortilla strips, cheese and chopped cilantro.

Makes 4 to 6 servings

Japanese Noodle Soup

1 package (8½ ounces) Japanese udon noodles

1 teaspoon vegetable oil

1 medium red bell pepper, cut into thin strips

1 medium carrot, diagonally sliced

2 green onions, thinly sliced

2 cans (about 14 ounces each) fat-free reduced-sodium beef broth

1 cup water

1 teaspoon reduced-sodium soy sauce

½ teaspoon grated fresh ginger

½ teaspoon black pepper

2 cups thinly sliced fresh shiitake mushrooms, stems discarded

4 ounces daikon (Japanese radish), peeled and cut into thin strips

4 ounces firm tofu, drained and cut into ½-inch cubes

1. Cook noodles according to package directions, omitting salt; drain. Rinse; set aside.

2. Heat oil in large nonstick saucepan over medium-high heat. Add bell pepper, carrot and green onions; cook about 3 minutes or until slightly softened. Stir in broth, water, soy sauce, ginger and black pepper; bring to a boil. Add mushrooms, daikon and tofu; reduce heat and simmer 5 minutes.

3. Place noodles in serving dishes; ladle soup over noodles.

Makes 6 servings

Shantung Twin Mushroom Soup

1 package (1 ounce) dried shiitake mushrooms

2 teaspoons vegetable oil

1 large onion, coarsely chopped

2 cloves garlic, minced

2 cups sliced button mushrooms

2 cans (about 14 ounces each) fat-free reduced-sodium chicken broth

2 ounces cooked ham, cut into thin slivers

½ cup thinly sliced green onions

1 tablespoon dry sherry

1 tablespoon reduced-sodium soy sauce

1 tablespoon cornstarch

1. Place shiitake mushrooms in small bowl; cover with boiling water. Let stand 20 minutes or until tender. Rinse well. Drain, squeezing out excess water. Cut off and discard stems; slice caps.

2. Heat oil in large saucepan over medium heat. Add onion and garlic; cook 1 minute. Stir in shiitake and button mushrooms; cook 4 minutes, stirring occasionally.

3. Add broth; bring to a boil over high heat. Reduce heat to medium; simmer, covered, 15 minutes.

4. Stir in ham and green onions; cook until heated through. Combine sherry, soy sauce and cornstarch in small bowl; mix well and stir into soup. Cook 2 minutes or until soup is thickened, stirring occasionally.

Makes 6 servings

Hot and Sour Soup

1 package (1 ounce) dried shiitake mushrooms

4 ounces firm tofu, drained

4 cups chicken broth

3 tablespoons white vinegar

2 tablespoons soy sauce

½ to 1 teaspoon hot chili oil

¼ teaspoon white pepper

1 cup shredded cooked pork, chicken **or** turkey

½ cup drained canned bamboo shoots, cut into thin strips

3 tablespoons water

2 tablespoons cornstarch

1 egg white, lightly beaten

¼ cup thinly sliced green onions **or** chopped fresh cilantro

1 teaspoon dark sesame oil

1. Place mushrooms in small bowl; cover with boiling water. Let stand 20 minutes or until tender. Rinse well. Drain; squeezing out excess water. Cut off and discard stems; slice caps. Press tofu lightly between paper towels; cut into ½-inch squares or triangles.

2. Combine broth, vinegar, soy sauce, chili oil and white pepper in medium saucepan. Bring to a boil over high heat. Reduce heat to medium-low; simmer 2 minutes.

3. Stir in mushrooms, tofu, pork and bamboo shoots; cook and stir until heated through.

4. Stir water into cornstarch in small bowl until smooth. Stir into soup until blended. Cook and stir 4 minutes or until soup boils and thickens. Remove from heat.

5. Stirring constantly in one direction, slowly pour egg white in thin stream into soup. Stir in green onions and sesame oil. Ladle into soup bowls.

Makes 4 servings

Mediterranean Shrimp Soup

2 cans (about 14 ounces each) fat-free reduced-sodium chicken broth

1 can (about 14 ounces) diced tomatoes

1 can (8 ounces) tomato sauce

1 medium onion, chopped

½ medium green bell pepper, chopped

½ cup orange juice

½ cup dry white wine (optional)

1 jar (2½ ounces) sliced mushrooms

¼ cup sliced pitted black olives

2 cloves garlic, minced

1 teaspoon dried basil

2 bay leaves

¼ teaspoon whole fennel seeds, crushed

⅛ teaspoon black pepper

1 pound medium raw shrimp, peeled and deveined

Slow Cooker Directions

1. Place all ingredients except shrimp in slow cooker. Cover; cook on LOW 4 to 4½ hours or until vegetables are crisp-tender.

2. Stir in shrimp. Cover; cook 15 to 30 minutes or until shrimp are pink and opaque. Remove and discard bay leaves.

Makes 6 servings

NOTE: For a heartier soup, add 1 pound of firm white fish, such as cod or haddock, cut into 1-inch pieces. Add the fish to the slow cooker 45 minutes before serving. Cook, covered, on LOW.

North African Chicken Soup

¾ teaspoon paprika

½ teaspoon ground cumin

½ teaspoon ground allspice

½ teaspoon ground ginger

8 ounces boneless skinless chicken breasts, cut into bite-size pieces

2½ cups fat-free reduced-sodium chicken broth

2 cups peeled sweet potato, cut into ½-inch pieces

1 cup chopped onion

½ cup water

3 cloves garlic, minced

1 teaspoon sugar

2 cups undrained canned tomatoes, cut up

Black pepper

1. Combine paprika, cumin, allspice and ginger in small bowl. Toss 1 teaspoon spice mixture with chicken pieces.

2. Spray large saucepan with olive oil cooking spray. Heat over medium-high heat. Add chicken; cook and stir 3 to 4 minutes or until chicken is cooked through. Remove to plate.

3. Combine broth, sweet potato, onion, water, garlic, sugar and remaining spice mixture in same saucepan; bring to a boil over high heat. Reduce heat and simmer, covered, 10 minutes or until sweet potato is tender. Stir in tomatoes and chicken; heat through. Season to taste with pepper.

Makes 4 servings

Spicy Thai Coconut Soup

2 cups chicken broth

1 can (13½ ounces) light coconut milk

1 tablespoon minced fresh ginger

½ to 1 teaspoon red curry paste

3 cups coarsely shredded cooked chicken (about 12 ounces)

1 can (15 ounces) straw mushrooms, drained

1 can (about 8 ounces) baby corn, drained

2 tablespoons lime juice

¼ cup chopped fresh cilantro

Combine broth, coconut milk, ginger and red curry paste in large saucepan. Add chicken, mushrooms and corn. Bring to a simmer over medium heat; cook until heated through. Stir in lime juice. Sprinkle with cilantro before serving.

Makes 4 servings

NOTE: Red curry paste can be found in jars in the Asian food section of large grocery stores. Spice levels can vary between brands. Start with ½ teaspoon, then add more as desired.

Wonton Soup

4 ounces ground pork, chicken or turkey

¼ cup finely chopped water chestnuts

2 tablespoons soy sauce, divided

1 egg white, lightly beaten

1 teaspoon minced fresh ginger

12 wonton wrappers

6 cups chicken broth

1½ cups spinach, torn

1 cup thinly sliced cooked pork (optional)

½ cup diagonally sliced green onions

1 tablespoon dark sesame oil

Shredded carrot (optional)

1. Combine ground pork, water chestnuts, 1 tablespoon soy sauce, egg white and ginger in small bowl; mix well.

2. Arrange wonton wrappers on clean work surface. Spoon 1 teaspoon filling near bottom point. Fold bottom point of wrapper up over filling; fold side points over filling. Moisten inside edges with water. Bring edges together firmly to seal. Repeat with remaining wrappers and filling.* Keep finished wontons covered with plastic wrap while filling remaining wrappers.

3. Combine broth and remaining 1 tablespoon soy sauce in large saucepan. Bring to a boil over high heat. Reduce heat to medium; add wontons. Simmer 4 minutes or until filling is cooked through.

4. Stir in spinach, sliced pork, if desired, and green onions; remove from heat. Stir in sesame oil. Ladle soup into bowls; garnish with shredded carrot.

Wontons may be made ahead to this point; cover and refrigerate up to 8 hours or freeze up to 3 months. Proceed as directed above if using refrigerated wontons; increase simmering time to 6 minutes if using frozen wontons.

Makes 4 servings

Ribollita (Tuscan Bread Soup)

2 tablespoons olive oil

1 onion, halved and thinly sliced

2 stalks celery, diced

1 large carrot, julienned

3 cloves garlic, minced

2 medium zucchini, halved lengthwise and thinly sliced

1 medium yellow squash, halved lengthwise and thinly sliced

1 can (28 ounces) whole tomatoes, undrained

1 can (about 15 ounces) cannellini beans, rinsed and drained

1½ teaspoons salt

1 teaspoon Italian seasoning

¼ teaspoon black pepper

1 bay leaf

¼ teaspoon red pepper flakes (optional)

4 cups vegetable broth

2 cups water

1 bunch kale, stemmed and coarsely chopped *or* 3 cups thinly sliced cabbage

8 ounces Tuscan or other rustic bread, cubed

Shredded Parmesan cheese (optional)

1. Heat oil in large saucepan over medium-high heat. Add onion, celery and carrot; cook and stir 5 minutes. Add garlic, zucchini and yellow squash; cook and stir 5 minutes. Add tomatoes, beans, salt, Italian seasoning, black pepper, bay leaf and red pepper flakes, if desired. Add broth and water; bring to a boil. Reduce heat; simmer 15 minutes. Add kale and bread; simmer 10 minutes or until vegetables are tender, bread is soft and soup is thick.

2. Top with Parmesan cheese just before serving.

Makes 6 to 8 servings

NOTE: This is a great recipe to use a spiralizer if you have one. Use the spiral slicing blade to spiral the zucchini and yellow squash, then cut in half to make half moon slices. Use the thin ribbon blade to spiral the onion and carrot, and then cut into desired lengths.

SLOW COOKER

Slow-Cooked French Onion Soup

4 tablespoons (½ stick) butter

3 large yellow onions, sliced

1 cup dry white wine

3 cans (about 14 ounces each) beef or chicken broth

1 teaspoon Worcestershire sauce

½ teaspoon salt

½ teaspoon dried thyme

4 slices French bread, toasted

1 cup (4 ounces) shredded Swiss cheese

Fresh thyme (optional)

1. Melt butter in large skillet over medium heat. Add onions, cook and stir 15 minutes or until onions are soft and lightly browned. Stir in wine.

2. Combine onion mixture, broth, Worcestershire sauce, salt and dried thyme in slow cooker. Cover; cook on LOW 4 to 4½ hours.

3. Ladle soup into 4 bowls; top each with bread slice and cheese. Garnish with fresh thyme.

Makes 4 servings

Country Turkey and Veggie Soup with Cream

2 tablespoons butter, divided

8 ounces sliced mushrooms

½ cup chopped onion

½ cup thinly sliced celery

1 red bell pepper, chopped

1 carrot, thinly sliced

½ teaspoon dried thyme

4 cups reduced-sodium chicken or turkey broth

4 ounces uncooked egg noodles

2 cups chopped cooked turkey

1 cup half-and-half

½ cup frozen peas, thawed

¾ teaspoon salt

1. Melt 1 tablespoon butter in large nonstick skillet over medium-high heat. Add mushrooms and onion; cook and stir 4 minutes or until onion is translucent. Transfer mixture to slow cooker.

2. Add celery, bell pepper, carrot and thyme to slow cooker; pour in broth. Cover; cook on HIGH 2½ hours.

3. Add noodles and turkey. Cover; cook on HIGH 20 minutes. Stir in half-and-half, peas, remaining 1 tablespoon butter and salt. Cook until noodles are tender and soup is heated through.

Makes 8 servings

Butternut Squash-Apple Soup

3 packages (12 ounces each) frozen cooked winter squash, thawed and drained **or** about 4½ cups mashed cooked butternut squash

2 cans (about 14 ounces each) chicken broth

1 medium Golden Delicious apple, peeled, cored and chopped

2 tablespoons minced onion

1 tablespoon packed brown sugar

1 teaspoon minced fresh sage **or** ½ teaspoon ground sage

¼ teaspoon ground ginger

½ cup whipping cream **or** half-and-half

1. Combine squash, broth, apple, onion, brown sugar, sage and ginger in slow cooker.

2. Cover; cook on LOW 6 hours or on HIGH 3 hours or until squash is tender.

3. Working in batches, pour soup into food processor or blender; process. Stir in cream just before serving.

Makes 6 to 8 servings

TIP: For thicker soup, use only 3 cups chicken broth.

Roasted Tomato-Basil Soup

2 cans (28 ounces each) whole tomatoes, drained and juice reserved (about 3 cups juice)

2½ tablespoons packed dark brown sugar

1 onion, finely chopped

3 cups chicken broth

3 tablespoons tomato paste

¼ teaspoon ground allspice

1 can (5 ounces) evaporated milk

¼ cup chopped fresh basil

Salt and black pepper

Additional fresh basil (optional)

Onion slices (optional)

1. Preheat oven to 450°F. Line baking sheet with foil; spray with nonstick cooking spray. Arrange tomatoes on foil in single layer. Sprinkle with brown sugar; top with onion. Bake 25 to 30 minutes or until tomatoes look dry and are lightly browned. Let tomatoes cool slightly; finely chop.

2. Place tomato mixture, 3 cups reserved juice from tomatoes, broth, tomato paste and allspice in slow cooker; mix well. Cover; cook on LOW 8 hours or on HIGH 4 hours.

3. Add evaporated milk and chopped basil; season with salt and pepper. Cook on HIGH 30 minutes or until heated through. Garnish with basil and onion slices.

Makes 6 servings

Tuscan White Bean Soup

10 cups chicken broth

1 package (16 ounces) dried Great Northern beans, rinsed and sorted

1 can (about 14 ounces) diced tomatoes

1 large onion, chopped

3 carrots, chopped

6 ounces bacon, crisp-cooked and diced

4 cloves garlic, minced

1 sprig fresh rosemary **or** 1 teaspoon dried rosemary

1 teaspoon black pepper

1. Combine broth, beans, tomatoes, onion, carrots, bacon, garlic, rosemary and pepper in 5-quart slow cooker.

2. Cover; cook on LOW 8 hours. Remove and discard rosemary before serving.

Makes 8 to 10 servings

SERVING SUGGESTION: Place slices of toasted Italian bread in soup bowls; drizzle with olive oil. Ladle soup over bread.

Hearty Mushroom and Barley Soup

9 cups chicken broth

1 package (16 ounces) sliced fresh mushrooms

1 onion, chopped

2 carrots, chopped

2 stalks celery, chopped

½ cup uncooked pearl barley

½ ounce dried porcini mushrooms

3 cloves garlic, minced

1 teaspoon salt

½ teaspoon dried thyme

½ teaspoon black pepper

Combine broth, sliced mushrooms, onion, carrots, celery, barley, porcini mushrooms, garlic, salt, thyme and pepper in 5-quart slow cooker. Cover; cook on LOW 4 to 6 hours.

Makes 8 to 10 servings

VARIATION: For even more flavor, add a beef or ham bone to the slow cooker with the rest of the ingredients.

Rich and Hearty Drumstick Soup

2 turkey drumsticks (about 1¾ pounds)

3 carrots, sliced

3 stalks celery, thinly sliced

1 onion, chopped

2 cloves garlic, minced

1 teaspoon poultry seasoning

4 cups reduced-sodium chicken broth

3 cups water

8 ounces uncooked egg noodles

⅓ cup chopped fresh Italian parsley

Salt and black pepper

1. Combine drumsticks, carrots, celery, onion, garlic and poultry seasoning in slow cooker. Pour broth and water over top. Cover; cook on HIGH 5 hours or until meat is falling off the bones.

2. Remove turkey; set aside. Add noodles to slow cooker. Cover; cook 30 minutes or until tender. Meanwhile, remove and discard skin and bones from turkey; shred meat.

3. Return turkey to slow cooker. Cover; cook until heated through. Stir in parsley. Season with salt and pepper.

Makes 8 servings

Smoked Sausage and Navy Bean Soup

8 cups chicken broth

1 package (16 ounces) dried navy beans, rinsed and sorted

2 ham hocks (about 1 pound total)

2 onions, diced

1 cup diced carrots

1 cup diced celery

1 can (about 14 ounces) diced tomatoes, undrained

2 tablespoons tomato paste

2 cloves garlic, minced

1 bay leaf

1 teaspoon dried thyme

1 pound smoked sausage, cut into ½-inch rounds

1. Bring broth to a boil in large saucepan over medium-high heat. Cover; reduce heat to low.

2. Place beans in 6-quart slow cooker. Add ham hocks, onions, carrots, celery, tomatoes, tomato paste, garlic, bay leaf and thyme. Carefully pour in hot broth. Cover; cook on HIGH 8 to 9 hours or until beans are tender.

3. Remove and discard bay leaf. Remove ham hocks; let stand until cool enough to handle. Remove ham from hocks; chop and return to slow cooker. Stir in sausage. Cover; cook 15 to 30 minutes or until sausage is heated through.

Makes 8 servings

Creamy Farmhouse Chicken and Garden Soup

½ package (16 ounces) frozen stir-fry vegetables

1 cup frozen corn, thawed

1 zucchini, sliced

2 bone-in chicken thighs, skinned*

1 can (about 14 ounces) chicken broth

½ teaspoon minced garlic

½ teaspoon dried thyme

2 ounces uncooked egg noodles

1 cup half-and-half

½ cup frozen peas

2 tablespoons finely chopped fresh parsley

2 tablespoons butter

1 teaspoon salt

½ teaspoon black pepper

To skin chicken easily, grasp skin with paper towel and pull away. Repeat with fresh paper towel for each piece of chicken, discarding skins and towels.

1. Combine stir-fry vegetables, corn and zucchini in slow cooker. Add chicken, broth, garlic and thyme. Cover; cook on HIGH 3 to 4 hours or until chicken is no longer pink in center. Remove chicken; cool slightly.

2. Add noodles to slow cooker. Cover; cook 20 minutes or until noodles are almost tender.

3. Meanwhile, debone and chop chicken. Return to slow cooker. Stir in half-and-half, peas, parsley, butter, salt and pepper. Let stand 5 minutes before serving.

Makes 4 servings

Curried Sweet Potato and Carrot Soup

2 sweet potatoes, peeled and cut into ¾-inch cubes (about 5 cups)

2 cups baby carrots

1 onion, chopped

¾ teaspoon curry powder

½ teaspoon salt

½ teaspoon black pepper

½ teaspoon ground cinnamon

¼ teaspoon ground ginger

4 cups chicken broth

¾ cup half-and-half

1 tablespoon maple syrup

Candied ginger (optional)

1. Place sweet potatoes, carrots, onion, curry powder, salt, pepper, cinnamon and ground ginger in slow cooker. Add broth. Stir well to combine. Cover; cook on LOW 7 to 8 hours.

2. Working in batches, process soup in blender or food processor until smooth. Return to slow cooker. (Or use immersion blender.) Add half-and-half and maple syrup. **Turn slow cooker to HIGH**. Cover; cook 15 minutes or until heated through. Garnish with candied ginger.

Makes 8 servings

TIP: For richer flavor, add a teaspoon of chicken soup base along with broth.

Double Corn Chowder

1 cup corn

1 cup canned hominy

6 ounces Canadian bacon, chopped

2 stalks celery, chopped

1 small onion or large shallot, chopped

1 jalapeño pepper,* seeded and minced

¼ teaspoon salt

¼ teaspoon dried thyme

¼ teaspoon black pepper

1 cup chicken broth

1 tablespoon all-purpose flour

1½ cups milk,** divided

Jalapeño peppers can sting and irritate the skin, so wear rubber gloves when handling peppers and do not touch your eyes.

**For richer chowder, use ¾ cup milk and ¾ cup half-and-half.*

1. Combine corn, hominy, bacon, celery, onion, jalapeño pepper, salt, thyme and black pepper in 4-quart slow cooker. Add broth. Cover; cook on LOW 5 to 6 hours or on HIGH 3 to 3½ hours.

2. Stir flour into 2 tablespoons milk in small bowl until smooth; stir into slow cooker. Stir in remaining milk. Cover; cook on LOW 20 minutes or until slightly thickened and heated through.

Makes 4 servings

Italian Hillside Garden Soup

1 tablespoon olive oil

1 cup chopped onion

1 cup chopped green bell pepper

½ cup sliced celery

2 cans (about 14 ounces each) chicken broth

1 can (about 15 ounces) navy beans, rinsed and drained

1 can (about 14 ounces) diced tomatoes with basil, garlic and oregano

1 medium zucchini, chopped

1 cup frozen cut green beans, thawed

¼ teaspoon garlic powder

1 package (9 ounces) refrigerated sausage- or cheese-filled tortellini

3 tablespoons chopped fresh basil

Grated Asiago or Parmesan cheese (optional)

1. Heat oil in large skillet over medium-high heat. Add onion, bell pepper and celery; cook and stir 4 minutes or until onion is translucent. Transfer to slow cooker.

2. Add broth, navy beans, tomatoes, zucchini, green beans and garlic powder. Cover; cook on LOW 7 hours or on HIGH 3½ hours.

3. Add tortellini; cook on HIGH 20 minutes or until pasta is tender. Stir in basil. Sprinkle with cheese, if desired, just before serving.

Makes 6 servings

No-Chop Black Bean Soup

3   cans (about 15 ounces each)
     black beans, rinsed and drained

1   package (12 ounces) frozen diced
     green bell peppers, thawed

2   cups frozen chopped onions,
     thawed

2   cans (about 14 ounces each)
     fat-free or regular chicken broth

1   can (about 14 ounces) diced
     tomatoes with pepper, celery
     and onion, undrained

1   teaspoon bottled minced garlic

1½ teaspoons ground cumin, divided

2   tablespoons olive oil

¾   teaspoon salt

1. Combine beans, bell peppers, onions, broth, tomatoes with juice, garlic and 1 teaspoon cumin in 4- to 5-quart slow cooker.

2. Cover; cook on LOW 8 to 10 hours or on HIGH 4 to 5 hours.

3. Stir in oil, salt and remaining ½ teaspoon cumin just before serving.

Makes 8 servings

Simple Turkey Soup

2 pounds ground turkey, cooked and drained

1 can (28 ounces) whole tomatoes, undrained

2 cans (about 14 ounces each) beef broth

1 package (16 ounces) frozen mixed soup vegetables (such as carrots, beans, okra, corn or onion), thawed

½ cup uncooked barley

1 teaspoon salt

1 teaspoon dried thyme

½ teaspoon ground coriander

Black pepper

Combine all ingredients in 5-quart slow cooker. Add water to cover. Cover; cook on HIGH 3 to 4 hours.

Makes 8 servings

TIP: Very easy to make. Try adding other frozen or canned vegetables or extra diced potatoes and carrots. Sliced, diced or stewed tomatoes can be substituted for the whole tomatoes. For a large crowd, add corn and serve with corn bread.

Celery-Leek Bisque with Basil

3 bunches leeks (3 pounds), trimmed and well rinsed*

2 cans (about 14 ounces each) 99% fat-free chicken broth

2 stalks celery, sliced

1 carrot, peeled and sliced (3 ounces)

3 cloves garlic, minced

1 cup cream cheese with garlic and herbs

2 cups half-and-half, plus additional for garnish

Salt and black pepper

Fresh basil leaves (optional)

Thoroughly rinsing the leeks is very important. Gritty sand can get between the layers of the leeks and can be difficult to see, so you may need to rinse them several times.

1. Combine leeks, broth, celery, carrot and garlic in 3½-to 4-quart slow cooker. Cover; cook on LOW 8 hours or on HIGH 4 hours.

2. Working in batches, process soup in blender or food processor until smooth. Add cream cheese to last batch. Return to slow cooker. Stir in half-and-half. Season with salt and pepper. For best flavor, cool to room temperature and refrigerate overnight. Reheat in large saucepan over medium heat before serving. Garnish with swirl of half-and-half and basil.

Makes 4 to 6 servings

Pumpkin Soup with Crumbled Bacon and Toasted Pumpkin Seeds

2 teaspoons olive oil

½ cup raw pumpkin seeds (pepitas)

1 onion, chopped

1 teaspoon coarse salt

½ teaspoon chipotle chili powder

½ teaspoon black pepper

2 cans (29 ounces each) solid-pack pumpkin

4 cups chicken stock or broth

¾ cup apple cider

½ cup whipping cream

Sour cream (optional)

3 slices thick-cut bacon, crisp-cooked and crumbled

1. Heat oil in medium skillet over medium heat. Add pumpkin seeds; cook and stir about 1 minute or until seeds begin to pop. Remove to small bowl; set aside.

2. Add onion to same skillet; cook and stir over medium heat until translucent. Stir in salt, chipotle powder and black pepper. Transfer to slow cooker. Stir in pumpkin, stock and cider until well blended. Cover; cook on HIGH 4 hours.

3. Turn off slow cooker. Stir in cream and adjust seasoning. Strain soup for smoother texture, if desired. Garnish with sour cream, toasted pumpkin seeds and bacon.

Makes 4 to 6 servings

TIP: Pumpkin seeds (or "pepitas") are a common ingredient in Mexican cooking. They can be purchased raw or roasted and salted; either variety may be found hulled or whole.

Shrimp and Pepper Bisque

1 bag (12 ounces) frozen stir-fry vegetables, thawed

½ pound frozen cauliflower florets, thawed

1 stalk celery, sliced

1 tablespoon seafood seasoning

½ teaspoon dried thyme

1 can (about 14 ounces) 99% fat-free chicken broth

12 ounces medium raw shrimp, peeled and deveined

2 cups half-and-half

2 to 3 green onions, finely chopped

1. Combine stir-fry vegetables, cauliflower, celery, seafood seasoning and thyme in 3½ to 4-quart slow cooker. Pour in broth. Cover; cook on LOW 8 hours or on HIGH 4 hours.

2. Stir in shrimp. Cover; cook 15 minutes or until shrimp are pink and opaque. Working in batches, process soup in food processor until smooth.

3. Return soup to slow cooker. Stir in half-and-half; cook until heated through. Sprinkle with green onions just before serving.

Makes 4 servings

TIP: For a creamier, smoother consistency, strain through several layers of damp cheesecloth.

Creamy Cauliflower Bisque

1 pound frozen cauliflower florets, thawed

1 pound russet potatoes, peeled and cut into 1-inch cubes

2 cans (about 14 ounces each) fat-free reduced-sodium chicken broth

1 cup chopped yellow onion

½ teaspoon dried thyme

¼ teaspoon garlic powder

⅛ teaspoon ground red pepper

1 cup fat-free evaporated milk

2 tablespoons butter

½ teaspoon salt

¼ teaspoon black pepper

1 cup (4 ounces) shredded reduced-fat sharp Cheddar cheese

¼ cup finely chopped fresh parsley

¼ cup finely chopped green onions

1. Layer cauliflower, potatoes, broth, onion, thyme, garlic powder and red pepper in 4-quart slow cooker. Cover; cook on LOW 8 hours or on HIGH 4 hours.

2. Working in batches, process soup in blender or food processor until smooth; return to slow cooker. Add evaporated milk, butter, salt and black pepper. Cook, uncovered, on HIGH 30 minutes or until heated through.

3. Ladle into bowls. Top each serving with cheese, parsley and green onions.

Makes 9 servings

Country Sausage and Bean Soup

2 cans (about 14 ounces each) reduced-sodium chicken broth

1½ cups hot water

1 cup dried black beans, rinsed and sorted

1 cup chopped yellow onion

2 bay leaves

1 teaspoon sugar

⅛ teaspoon ground red pepper

6 ounces bulk pork sausage

1 cup chopped tomato

1 tablespoon chili powder

1 tablespoon Worcestershire sauce

2 teaspoons olive oil

1½ teaspoons ground cumin

½ teaspoon salt

¼ cup chopped fresh cilantro

1. Combine broth, water, beans, onion, bay leaves, sugar and red pepper in slow cooker. Cover; cook on LOW 8 hours or on HIGH 4 hours.

2. Brown sausage in large skillet over medium heat, stirring to break up meat. Drain fat.

3. Add sausage, tomato, chili powder, Worcestershire sauce, oil, cumin and salt to slow cooker. Cover; cook on HIGH 15 minutes. Remove and discard bay leaves. Ladle soup into bowls; sprinkle with cilantro.

Makes 9 servings

Minestrone alla Milanese

2 cans (about 14 ounces each) reduced-sodium beef broth

1 can (about 14 ounces) diced tomatoes, undrained

1 cup diced potato

1 cup coarsely chopped carrots

1 cup coarsely chopped green cabbage

1 cup sliced zucchini

¾ cup chopped onion

¾ cup sliced fresh green beans

¾ cup coarsely chopped celery

¾ cup water

2 tablespoons olive oil

1 clove garlic, minced

½ teaspoon dried basil

¼ teaspoon dried rosemary

1 bay leaf

1 can (about 15 ounces) cannellini beans, rinsed and drained

Shredded Parmesan cheese (optional)

1. Combine all ingredients except cannellini beans and cheese in 5-quart slow cooker; mix well. Cover; cook on LOW 5 to 6 hours.

2. Add cannellini beans. Cover; cook on LOW 1 hour or until vegetables are tender.

3. Remove and discard bay leaf. Garnish with cheese.

Makes 8 to 10 servings

Beer and Cheese Soup

1 can (about 14 ounces) chicken broth

1 cup beer

¼ cup finely chopped onion

2 cloves garlic, minced

¾ teaspoon dried thyme

1½ cups (6 ounces) shredded American cheese

1½ cups (6 ounces) shredded sharp Cheddar cheese

1 cup milk

½ teaspoon paprika

2 to 3 slices pumpernickel or rye bread

1. Combine broth, beer, onion, garlic and thyme in slow cooker. Cover; cook on LOW 4 hours.

2. **Turn slow cooker to HIGH.** Stir in cheeses, milk and paprika. Cover; cook on HIGH 45 to 60 minutes or until heated through.

3. Meanwhile, preheat oven to 425°F. Cut bread into ½-inch cubes; place on small baking sheet. Bake 10 to 12 minutes or until crisp, stirring once. Serve croutons with soup.

Makes 4 servings

Campfire Sausage and Potato Soup

8 ounces kielbasa sausage

1 large baking potato, cut into ½-inch cubes

1 can (about 15 ounces) dark red kidney beans, rinsed and drained

1 can (about 14 ounces) diced tomatoes

1 can (10½ ounces) condensed beef broth

1 medium onion, diced

1 medium green bell pepper, diced

1 teaspoon dried oregano

½ teaspoon sugar

1 to 2 teaspoons ground cumin

1. Cut sausage lengthwise in half, then crosswise into ½-inch pieces. Combine sausage, potato, beans, tomatoes, broth, onion, bell pepper, oregano and sugar in slow cooker.

2. Cover; cook on LOW 8 hours or on HIGH 4 hours.

3. Season with cumin before serving.

Makes 6 to 7 servings

Chicken and Wild Rice Soup

3 cans (about 14 ounces each) chicken broth

1 pound boneless skinless chicken breasts or thighs, cut into bite-size pieces

2 cups water

1 cup sliced celery

1 cup diced carrots

1 package (6 ounces) converted long grain and wild rice mix with seasoning packet (not quick-cooking or instant rice)

½ cup chopped onion

½ teaspoon black pepper

2 teaspoons white vinegar (optional)

1 tablespoon dried parsley flakes

1. Combine broth, chicken, water, celery, carrots, rice with seasoning packet, onion and pepper in slow cooker; mix well.

2. Cover; cook on LOW 6 to 7 hours or on HIGH 4 to 5 hours or until chicken is tender.

3. Stir in vinegar, if desired. Sprinkle with parsley.

Makes 9 servings

Potato & Spinach Soup with Gouda

6 cups cubed peeled Yukon Gold potatoes (about 9 medium)

2 cans (about 14 ounces each) chicken broth

½ cup water

1 small red onion, finely chopped

5 ounces baby spinach

½ teaspoon salt

¼ teaspoon ground red pepper

¼ teaspoon black pepper

2½ cups (10 ounces) shredded smoked Gouda cheese, divided

1 can (12 ounces) evaporated milk

1 tablespoon olive oil

4 cloves garlic, cut into thin slices

Chopped fresh parsley

1. Combine potatoes, broth, water, onion, spinach, salt, red pepper and black pepper in slow cooker. Cover; cook on LOW 10 hours or on HIGH 4 to 5 hours.

2. Slightly mash potatoes in slow cooker; add 2 cups cheese and evaporated milk. Cover; cook on HIGH 15 to 20 minutes or until cheese is melted.

3. Heat oil in small skillet over low heat. Add garlic; cook and stir 2 minutes or until golden brown. Remove from heat. Sprinkle soup with garlic, remaining ½ cup cheese and parsley.

Makes 8 to 10 servings

TIP: Yukon Gold potatoes are thin-skinned, pale yellow-gold potatoes with pale yellow flesh. When buying potatoes, make sure there are no bruises, sprouts or green areas. Store Yukon Golds in a cool, dark place and use within 1 week of purchase.

Beef Fajita Soup

1   pound beef stew meat

1   can (about 15 ounces) pinto beans, rinsed and drained

1   can (about 15 ounces) black beans, rinsed and drained

1   can (about 14 ounces) diced tomatoes with roasted garlic

1   can (about 14 ounces) beef broth

1½ cups water

1   green bell pepper, thinly sliced

1   red bell pepper, thinly sliced

1   onion, thinly sliced

2   teaspoons ground cumin

1   teaspoon seasoned salt

1   teaspoon black pepper

Toppings: sour cream, shredded Monterey Jack or Cheddar cheese, chopped olives

1. Combine beef, beans, tomatoes, broth, water, bell peppers, onion, cumin, seasoned salt and black pepper in slow cooker.

2. Cover; cook on LOW 8 hours.

3. Serve with desired toppings.

Makes 8 servings

Chicken & Barley Soup

1   cup thinly sliced celery

1   medium onion, coarsely chopped

1   carrot, thinly sliced

½   cup uncooked medium pearl
     barley

1   clove garlic, minced

1   cut-up whole chicken (about
     3 pounds)

1   tablespoon olive oil

2½ cups chicken broth

1   can (about 14 ounces) diced
     tomatoes

¾   teaspoon salt

½   teaspoon dried basil

¼   teaspoon black pepper

1. Place celery, onion, carrot, barley and garlic in slow cooker.

2. Remove and discard skin from chicken. Separate drumsticks from thighs. Trim back bone from breasts. Save wings for another use. Heat oil in large skillet over medium-high heat; brown chicken on all sides. Place in slow cooker.

3. Add broth, tomatoes, salt, basil and pepper to slow cooker. Cover; cook on LOW 7 to 8 hours or HIGH 4 hours or until chicken and barley are tender. Remove chicken from slow cooker; separate meat from bones. Cut into bite-size pieces, discarding bones; stir chicken into soup.

Makes 4 servings

Navy Bean & Ham Soup

6 cups water

5 cups dried navy beans, soaked overnight, rinsed and drained

1 pound ham, cubed

1 can (about 15 ounces) corn, drained

1 can (about 4 ounces) mild diced green chiles, drained

1 onion, diced

Salt and black pepper

1. Place water, beans, ham, corn, chiles, onion, salt and pepper in slow cooker.

2. Cover; cook on LOW 8 to 10 hours or until beans are softened.

Makes 6 servings

INDEX

METRIC CONVERSION CHART

VOLUME MEASUREMENTS (dry)

$\frac{1}{8}$ teaspoon = 0.5 mL
$\frac{1}{4}$ teaspoon = 1 mL
$\frac{1}{2}$ teaspoon = 2 mL
$\frac{3}{4}$ teaspoon = 4 mL
1 teaspoon = 5 mL
1 tablespoon = 15 mL
2 tablespoons = 30 mL
$\frac{1}{4}$ cup = 60 mL
$\frac{1}{3}$ cup = 75 mL
$\frac{1}{2}$ cup = 125 mL
$\frac{2}{3}$ cup = 150 mL
$\frac{3}{4}$ cup = 175 mL
1 cup = 250 mL
2 cups = 1 pint = 500 mL
3 cups = 750 mL
4 cups = 1 quart = 1 L

VOLUME MEASUREMENTS (fluid)

1 fluid ounce (2 tablespoons) = 30 mL
4 fluid ounces ($\frac{1}{2}$ cup) = 125 mL
8 fluid ounces (1 cup) = 250 mL
12 fluid ounces (1$\frac{1}{2}$ cups) = 375 mL
16 fluid ounces (2 cups) = 500 mL

WEIGHTS (mass)

$\frac{1}{2}$ ounce = 15 g
1 ounce = 30 g
3 ounces = 90 g
4 ounces = 120 g
8 ounces = 225 g
10 ounces = 285 g
12 ounces = 360 g
16 ounces = 1 pound = 450 g

DIMENSIONS

$\frac{1}{16}$ inch = 2 mm
$\frac{1}{8}$ inch = 3 mm
$\frac{1}{4}$ inch = 6 mm
$\frac{1}{2}$ inch = 1.5 cm
$\frac{3}{4}$ inch = 2 cm
1 inch = 2.5 cm

OVEN TEMPERATURES

250°F = 120°C
275°F = 140°C
300°F = 150°C
325°F = 160°C
350°F = 180°C
375°F = 190°C
400°F = 200°C
425°F = 220°C
450°F = 230°C

BAKING PAN SIZES

Utensil	Size in Inches/Quarts	Metric Volume	Size in Centimeters
Baking or Cake Pan (square or rectangular)	8×8×2	2 L	20×20×5
	9×9×2	2.5 L	23×23×5
	12×8×2	3 L	30×20×5
	13×9×2	3.5 L	33×23×5
Loaf Pan	8×4×3	1.5 L	20×10×7
	9×5×3	2 L	23×13×7
Round Layer Cake Pan	8×1½	1.2 L	20×4
	9×1½	1.5 L	23×4
Pie Plate	8×1¼	750 mL	20×3
	9×1¼	1 L	23×3
Baking Dish or Casserole	1 quart	1 L	—
	1½ quart	1.5 L	—
	2 quart	2 L	—